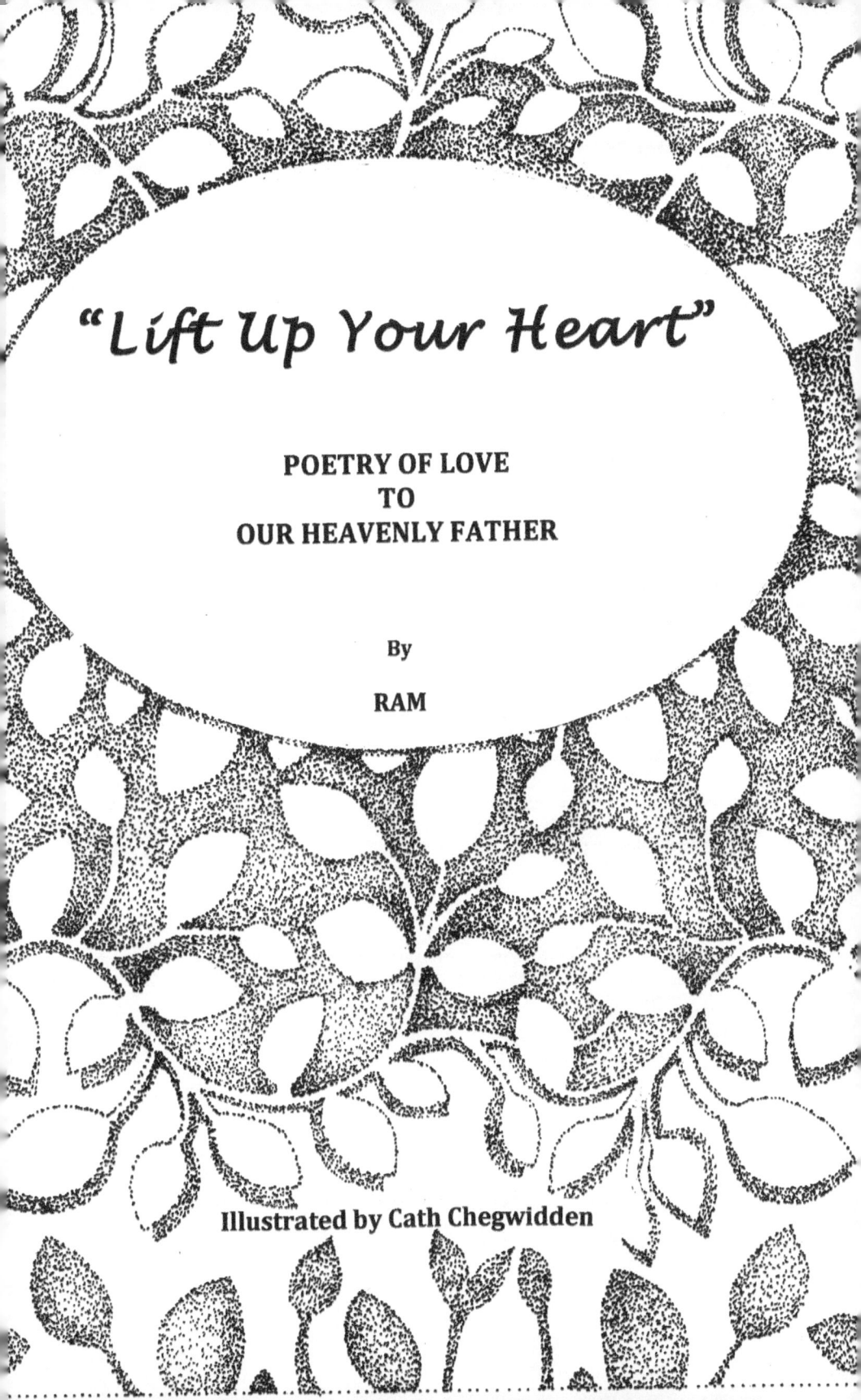

"Lift Up Your Heart"

**POETRY OF LOVE
TO
OUR HEAVENLY FATHER**

By

RAM

Illustrated by Cath Chegwidden

Copyright © 2018 by RAM.

Library of Congress Control Number: 2018911528
ISBN:
Hardcover 978-1-9845-0260-5
Softcover 978-1-9845-0259-9
eBook 978-1-9845-0258-2

All rights reserved. No part of this book may be reproduced or transmitted in any form or by any means, electronic or mechanical, including photocopying, recording, or by any information storage and retrieval system, without permission in writing from the copyright owner.

Contemporary English Version (CEV)
Copyright © 1995 by American Bible Society

New International Version (NIV)
Holy Bible, New International Version®, NIV® Copyright ©1973, 1978, 1984, 2011 by Biblica, Inc.® Used by permission. All rights reserved worldwide.

New Revised Standard Version (NRSV)
New Revised Standard Version Bible, copyright © 1989 the Division of Christian Education of the National Council of the Churches of Christ in the United States of America. Used by permission. All rights reserved.

Good News Translation (GNT)
Copyright © 1992 by American Bible Society

New Living Translation (NLT)
Holy Bible, New Living Translation, copyright © 1996, 2004, 2015 by Tyndale House Foundation. Used by permission of Tyndale House Publishers, Inc., Carol Stream, Illinois 60188. All rights reserved.

English Standard Version (ESV)
The Holy Bible, English Standard Version. ESV® Text Edition: 2016. Copyright © 2001 by Crossway Bibles, a publishing ministry of Good News Publishers.

King James Version (KJV)
Public Domain

Any people depicted in stock imagery provided by Getty Images are models, and such images are being used for illustrative purposes only.
Certain stock imagery © Getty Images.

Print information available on the last page.

Rev. date: 12/07/2018

To order additional copies of this book, contact:
Xlibris
1-800-455-039
www.Xlibris.com.au
Orders@Xlibris.com.au

To
God the Father Infinite Love and Wisdom
God the Son Eternal Redeemer
and Faithful Friend
God the Holy Spirit, Comforter,
Teacher and Guide.
For I would never have had the
inspiration to write this book
without the healing love placed
in my heart by Jesus Christ.

Soli Deo Gloria.
To the glory of God alone.

To my mother, Helen Edna Murray
who persevered with eight children
to take us to church and introduce us to Jesus.
Thank you Mum,
for the prayers, love, blood, sweat, and tears.
You have always been my inspiration
when the going gets tough
to keep on giving and not give
up a personal relationship
with God for the superficial
enticements of this world.
I love you.

The Foreword

The news that you are terminally ill with a particularly aggressive form of cancer is daunting for anyone. Everyone who experiences this loss of time to live and any feelings of control must face eternal questions about dying and the existence of heaven and a loving God.

Robyn A. McGuirk (RAM), with the diagnosis of metastatic cancer, was thrust suddenly into this cancer journey, but as a woman of deep Christian faith, she has an intimate and personal love of God to sustain her. She wasn't prepared to leave her loved ones without a fight or a uniquely special legacy. At first, she thought she would write a children's book. However, during the creation of this and her continuous chemotherapy treatments, she passed the time by composing the wonderful poetry that expresses her challenges, personal grief, and through it all, her love of God. Her writing has come together as this devotional and poetry book. Robyn continues to write stories and poetry.

My name is Cath Chegwidden, and I am an artist and illustrator. I first heard of Robyn while she was being interviewed on the Rhema 99.7 Christian radio station in Newcastle, New South Wales. As she related her circumstances in the interview and her need for a children's book illustrator, I felt God tap my shoulder. Being women of like faith and with her being a cancer survivor, ours was a partnership heaven sent. When we met, she brought both the rough draft of the children's book and her poetry. Immediately I was captivated by the sincerity of her poems, and they in turn inspired my illustrations.

The next stumbling block was to publish. This was a precious dream, and with medically exhausted financial resources, Robyn prayed that God would find a way for her. The prayers were answered by the wonderful Australian charity organization Dreams2Live4. Without this organization's support, the publication would not have been possible. This book then has become a testimony to her perseverance, faith, answered prayers, and God's wonderful provision.

This creative journey has, we believe, been inspired by God. The poems by Robyn and the complementary devotional reflections are a heart- and love-centred gift she hopes will help others in like journeys to feel unafraid and comforted. It has been composed that each person who reads it may learn that when tested by news of terminal illness, you are never alone. Surrender to Jesus. He'll be there for you.

Cath Chegwidden

Acknowledgements

To my husband, Tim, who is my dear friend, thank you for lovingly supporting me through this cancer journey. He listens to my poetry, helps with the housework, and cooks many dinners. Tim has been a great encouragement and loving strength and earthly support throughout this precious time. I love you.

A special thank you is extended to the Australian charity organization Dreams2Live4, which fulfils the dreams for people who are living with metastatic cancer.

I filled out an online application form and was informed by Louise, who administers there, that my dream had been granted. How exciting! It's a goal to aspire to, something to help me feel part of life, and now I'm becoming a published author! This has been a lengthy process, and Dreams2Live4 has supported me all the way.

Dreams2Live4, you have not only my gratitude and thanks but also the appreciation from all the dreamers who had their dreams realised. This book would not have been possible without Dreams2Live4, let me encourage all those who read this book, that is another dream that has come to fruition, to donate to this wonderful cause. Just go to www.Dreams2Live4.org.au, and read the inspiring stories of the dreamers and their realised dreams.

My thanks also go to Cath Chegwidden, who spent dedicated hours working on the illustrations. They are the fruit of many years as an art teacher, muralist, and illustrator, and they reflect Cath's indigenous heritage and Christian beliefs. Cath is now going on to study to become a chaplain.

Thank you to my dear friend Helen Scott for your cut-throat honesty in critiquing my writing. You have been a great help in keeping me focused and cutting out oversentimentality.

Contents

Poem		Devotional	
2	Song in My Heart	3	Sing Praise to the King of the Universe
4	Praise the LORD		
6	Take My Life	5	Peace at the Centre
8	God's Grand Design	7	Surrender All
10	Rain	9	God's Handwriting
12	Never Alone	11	Give God the Glory
14	One Day at a Time	13	God Is Everywhere
16	The Lonely Man	19	Masks Off
18	The Brave Face	21	What God's Love Means
20	The Gift	23	Everlasting Streams
22	The Fountain of Life	25	Ascribe Glory to the LORD
24	The Whisper of My Spirit	27	See the Light
26	Turn to Truth's Light	29	Taming the Tongue
28	The Rudderless Ship	31	From the LORD Comes Deliverance
30	Temptation		
32	Money	33	The Want of Money
34	The Pain of Separation	35	Hold Onto God
36	Please Come, Lord	37	God Will Rescue Us
38	Be Strong	39	Spiritually Strong
40	Rise Up with Jesus	41	Stand Tall with Faith in Your Heart
42	Behold, He's Knocking at Your Door	43	I Am the Door
44	The Armour of God	45	Spiritual Armour
46	Don't Delay	47	Remember Others
48	Don't Mourn for Me	49	The Promise of Eternal Life
50	The Mind of RAM	51	Wonderfully Made

The Introduction

The poetry in this book has come from within me, from feelings of great love and comfort to being alone, isolated, scared, and uncertain of my earthly future. After a diagnosis of terminal breast cancer, I found my feelings bleeding out into words.

There are times of deep trouble or sadness, when a person's life direction is completely changed by circumstances beyond their reach and it is out of their control. It is during these dark, lonely times—when one feels directionless, deserted by human compassion and understanding—that we need to know that there is a wonderful Saviour just waiting to lift us up. It is when we lose our human strength that the power of the Holy Spirit comes to comfort and guide us and bring us out the other end with a stronger belief and enduring faith.

As you read this collection of poetry and the accompanying powerful scriptural messages, may God reveal to you that you are far from being alone.

May you feel so close to the love of our Heavenly Father that you will be inspired, challenged, feel a greater peace, and know with certainty that your eternal home is secure.

Song in My Heart

I was born with a song in my heart given by my LORD
When I raise my voice in praise, that is enough reward
Although like an angel's voice, my song will never be
My song of love is sent above to sweet eternity

The love I feel is everywhere, in every tiny flower
A real and visible sign to me of God's majestic power
I have no need to run, hide or fight
My minds at peace, my souls made right

By the sacrifice of my Lord when dying on the cross
This He did to show me love in my trials and loss
I look to Him with a trusting heart as I sing for Him my song
And I know that He's travelling with me, my companion all along

Sing Praise to the King of the Universe

> Clap your hands all you nations, Shout to God with cries of Joy for the LORD Most High is awesome, the great King over all the earth. He subdued nations under us, peoples under our feet. He chose our inheritance for us, the pride of Jacob, whom he loved. God has ascended amid shouts of joy, the LORD amid the sounding of trumpets. Sing praises to God, sing praises; sing praises to our King, sing praises. For God is the King of all the earth; sing to him a psalm of praise. God reigns over the nations; God is seated on his holy throne. The nobles of the nations assemble as the people of the God of Abraham, for the kings of the earth belong to God; he is greatly exalted. Psalm 47, NIV

> He put a new song in my mouth, a hymn of Praise to our God. Many will see fear and put their trust in the LORD. Psalm 40:3, NIV

Our God is the King of the universe and loves us to sing our heartfelt praises to Him.

> For God is the King over all the earth: sing to Him a song of Praise. Psalm 47:7, NIV

We can often get caught up in worldly cares with pain, loss, and stress.

Singing brings joy to the heart and peace to the soul. We can lose ourselves in rapturous songs of praise to our King.

It's easy to feel sorry for ourselves, I have found that when I sing praises to God, it transforms the bleakest mood to appreciation and sunshine.

Fill your heart with song, make one up, sing in the car, sing quietly, sing loudly, sing out of key . . . Try it.

I have found that when holding a crying baby, if I start singing and persevere, the baby will usually stop crying, maybe subdued to a sob, but it lifts the gloom.

Put a smile on your face and a song in your heart today!

Praise the LORD

Praise the Lord oh my soul!
For He guides me and makes me whole
He satisfies my heart's desire
And raises me up and lifts me higher

To the beauty and life that flows from nature
Cleanses, frees, and attests to His grandeur
I don't care what tomorrow may bring
For with each day my heart will sing

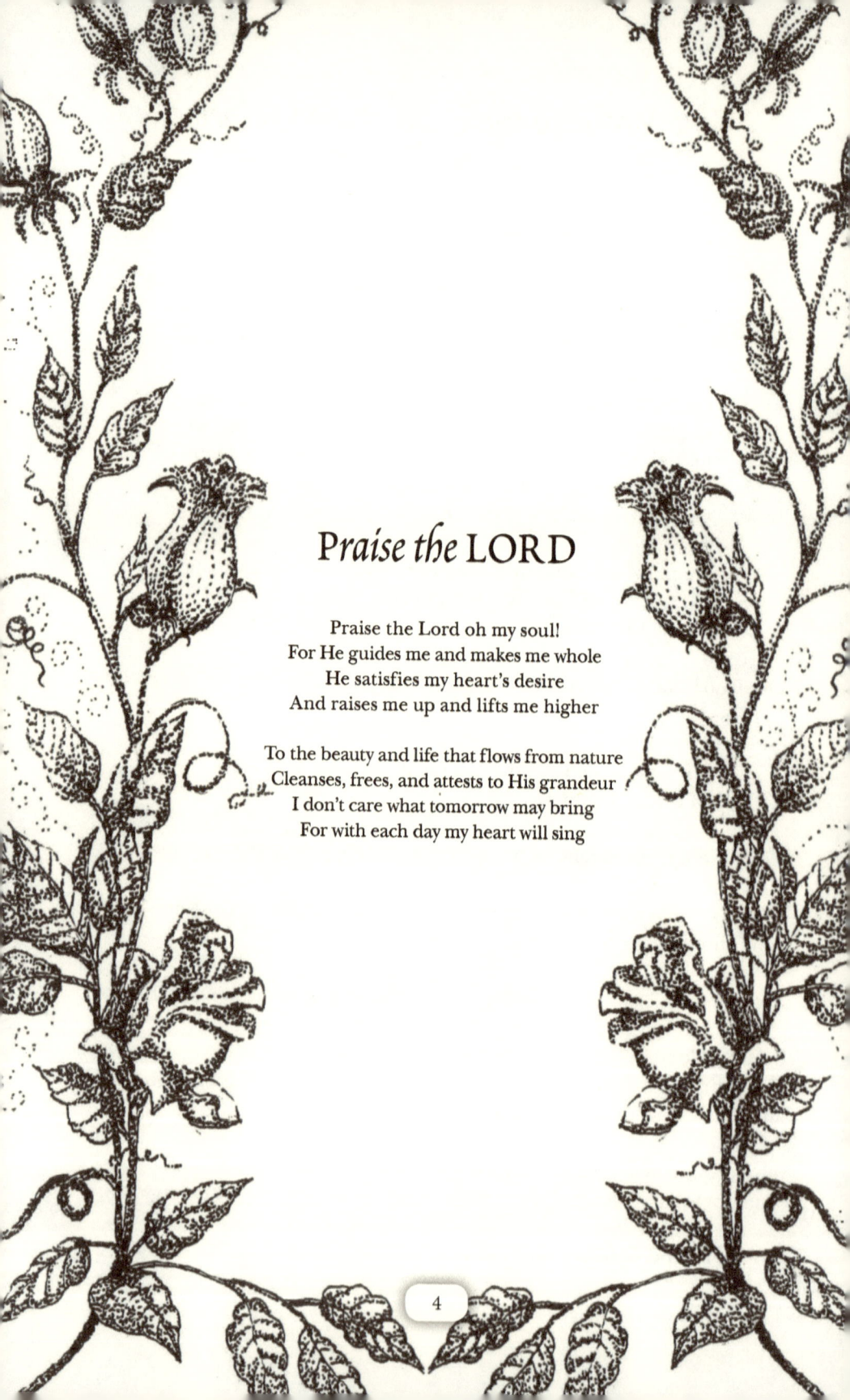

Peace at the Centre

Peace I leave with you; my peace I give you. I do not give to you as the world gives. Do not let your hearts be troubled and do not be afraid. John 14:27 NIV

Peace in your heart makes your life wonderful no matter the trials and struggles. It is this peace God gives when you draw close to Him to receive His love and blessing. This peace counters the turbulence you have elsewhere in your life. It brings the stability of knowing you belong to God and the security of knowing He is with you always.

God's peace comes when you know how much God loves you, how far He goes to forgive you, how many ways He sustains you, and how many generous life opportunities He offers you. God's peace will guide you in the way you should go.

"Do not be anxious about anything, but in every situation, by prayer and petition, with thanksgiving, present your requests to God. And the peace of God, which transcends all understanding, will guard your hearts and your minds in Christ Jesus." Philippians 4:6-7 NIV

The peace that Christ gives is to guide you in the decisions you make, for it is to this peace that God has called you together in one body. Colossians 3:15, GNT

God puts the calm of His presence and the peace of His love at the centre of your life.

"A heart at peace gives life to the body, but envy rots the bones" Proverbs 14:30, NIV

"You will keep in perfect peace those whose minds are steadfast, because they trust in you." Isaiah 26:3 NIV

"Love and faithfulness meet together; righteousness and peace kiss each other. Faithfulness springs forth from the earth, and righteousness looks down from heaven". Psalm 85:10-11, NIV

"For, whoever would love life and see good days must keep their tongue from evil and their lips from deceitful speech. They must turn from evil and do good; they must seek peace and pursue it." 1 Peter 3:10-11 NIV

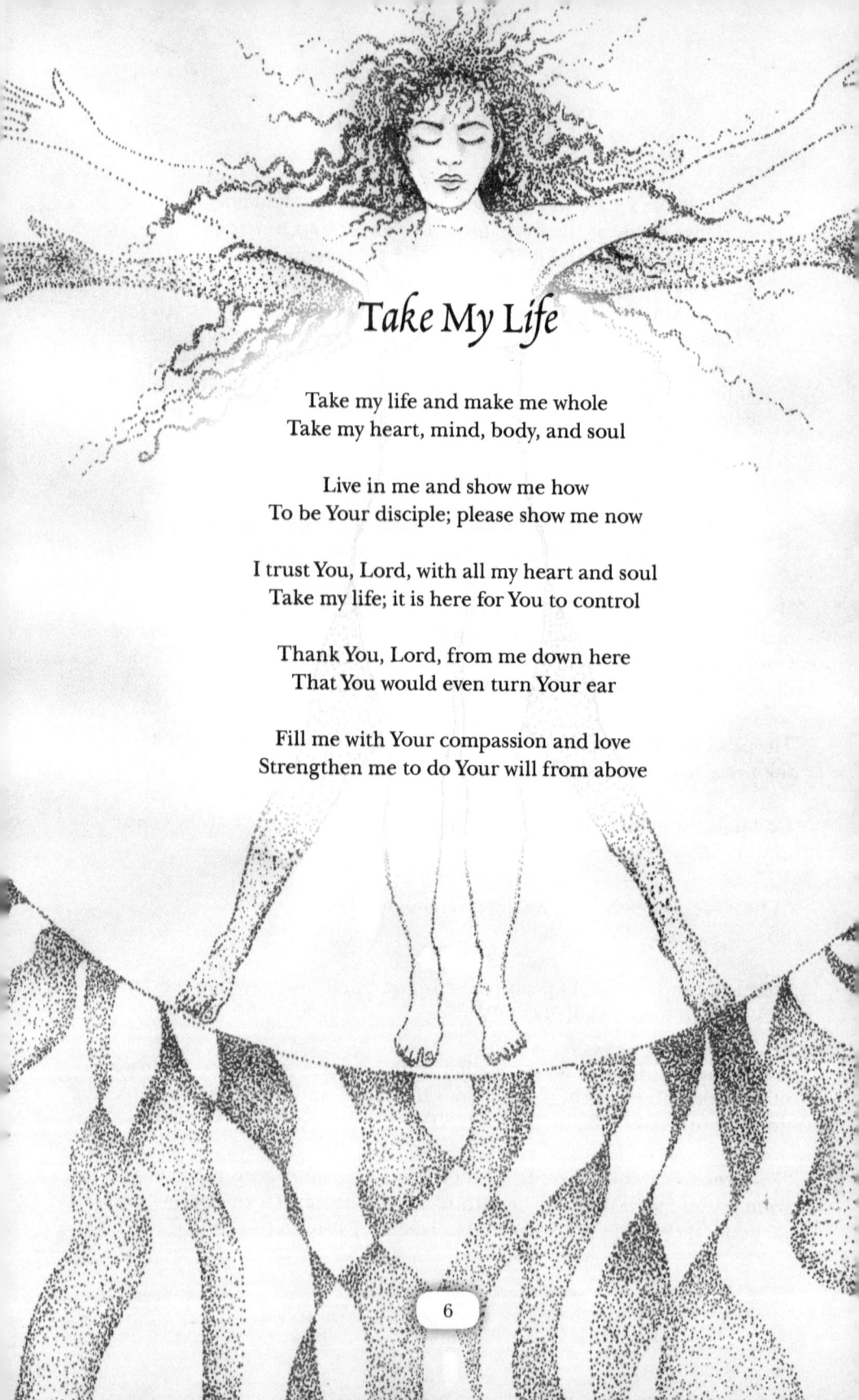

Take My Life

Take my life and make me whole
Take my heart, mind, body, and soul

Live in me and show me how
To be Your disciple; please show me now

I trust You, Lord, with all my heart and soul
Take my life; it is here for You to control

Thank You, Lord, from me down here
That You would even turn Your ear

Fill me with Your compassion and love
Strengthen me to do Your will from above

Surrender All

I trust in you, O LORD; I say, "You are my God," My times are in your hand...
Psalm 31:14-15 NRSV

Give your problems, challenges and difficulties to God unreservedly. Give God your situations willingly without disclaimer or condition, without reservation, give God your illness, your relationships, employment issues, and inner struggles. Give God all your troubles and say to Him "It's your call." I trust in you, O LORD; I say, "You are my God," My times are in your hand...

"The eyes of the LORD range throughout the earth to strengthen those whose hearts are fully committed to him." 2 Chronicles 16:9, NIV

Nothing about me is hidden from You! I was secretly woven together out of human sight, but with Your own eyes you saw my body being formed. Even before I was born, You had written in Your book everything about me. Psalm 139:15-16, CEV

There's no need to be scared to surrender, surrender all, all your worries and anxieties, sometimes things get worse before they get better, hang in there, remember the sufferings of Job, read his story and believe the great victory that he achieved is also available for you. Job knew he was not alone, he had Gods love in his heart.

"Then Job replied to the LORD: "I know that you can do all things; no purpose of yours can be thwarted. You asked, 'Who is this that obscures my plans without knowledge?' Surely, I spoke of things I did not understand, things too wonderful for me to know" Job 42:13, NIV

Trust and surrender ask, and the Holy Spirit will come to help you in any dire situation you find yourself in.

"I have been crucified with Christ and I no longer live, but Christ lives in me. The life I now live in the body, I live by faith in the Son of God, who loved me and gave himself for me" Galatians 2:20, NIV

Turn things over to God. He knows better what to do with them than you do. Let God carry you. He is better able to do that than you. It is letting go, not holding on, that makes you strong. It is coming to God with full hands and leaving with empty ones. Give control to God, Make Him the Lord of your life.

God's Grand Design

This grand design, developed
with the wisdom of time
Stupendous creations, shining light, source divine
Infinite treasures over all the earth do abound
The oceans, mountains, and rainforests all around

We cannot see with our limited sight
This grand design wrought by
God's grace and might
This treasure made finite by the foe of greed
Evils, perversion, the devil's seed

For fighting this foe, we all must do
Love God and others as He requires us to
Each action considered with the impact in mind
Have the desire to know Jesus, ask, seek, and find

With care and nurturing and God-sent power
The ego recedes, and the faith
filled will find power
His grand design continues; God's will be done
Until He has dominion, His victory won.

God's Handwriting

> The heavens keep telling the wonders of God, and the skies declare what he has done. Psalm 19:1, CEV

God has written His name everywhere. But you have to know what you're looking at. When the astronauts who participated in the moon landing in July 1969 were asked to contribute a written testimonial for a capsule that was to remain on the moon after they left, Buzz Aldrin chose the following words from Psalm 8:

> O LORD, our LORD,
> How majestic is your name in all the earth!
> You have set your glory
> Above the heavens . . .
> When I consider your heavens,
> The work of your fingers,
> The moon and the stars,
> Which you have set in place,
> What is man that you are mindful of him,
> The son of man that you care for him?
> You made him a little lower than the heavenly beings
> And crowned him with glory and honour.
> You made him ruler over the works of your hands;
> You put everything under his feet . . .
> O Lord, our Lord,
> How majestic is your name in all the earth.

When Neil Armstrong looked back at the earth from the lunar module, he raised his thumb and covered it. In doing so, he realized how truly tiny we all are in God's scheme of things. When you look for God's signature and know that is what you are doing, you will see it everywhere. Every place and every person exhibit's the handwriting of God. His name is everywhere.

Rain

Rain is so wonderful; it replenishes the earth
Giving flowers, trees, and plants new birth
After the hottest and dustiest of days
The rain comes along, and dust washes away

There is oppressive unseen fog all around
Hot sun bearing down, drying all the ground
Steamy air, heavy with a humid atmosphere
We just sit, praying for the rain to appear

Sitting with lathered sweat on our skin
Moisture trickles down and drips past our chins
The Aussie summer is all-pervading, the heat bearing down
Giving unprotected heads a shiny golden crown

The rain can come with a gentle touch
Or pour down in a furious rush
The droplets running down the windowpane
Hold the promise of new life again

Give God the Glory

> Hallelujah! It's a good thing to sing praise to our God; praise is beautiful, praise is fitting. Psalm 147:1, The Message

A cancer patient about to receive chemotherapy drugs intravenously always bowed his head and said grace before he did so. When questioned why he did this, he told them this was like food and was keeping him alive. He also noted that he thought of the many hands and minds that had made the drug available. He prayed for the researchers who conducted years of painstaking testing, the investors and companies who made the drug possible, the doctors and nurses who administered it, and the government subsidy that made supply accessible no matter your circumstances financially. When you think about it, those who bless us are often hidden behind an end product or outcome.

A minister had just started his Sunday sermon when thunder and lightning began to rumble and flash. Rain poured down in torrents. 'God is wonderful!' he told the congregation. 'While all of us are sitting here dry and comfortable, He's out there in the parking area, washing our cars for us!'

> "I will extol the LORD at all times; his praise will always be on my lips. I will glory in the LORD; let the afflicted hear and rejoice. Glorify the LORD with me; let us exalt his name together. I sought the LORD, and he answered me; he delivered me from all my fears." Psalm 34:1-4 NIV

> Find phrases for your praises. Create many and varied ways to say thank you to God. You can never say or sing enough praises to God.

> "Praise be to the LORD, the God of Israel, from everlasting to everlasting. Then all the people said "Amen" and "Praise the LORD." 1 Chronicles 16:36 NIV

> "David praised the LORD in the presence of the whole assembly, saying, "Praise be to you, LORD, the God of our father Israel, from everlasting to everlasting. Yours, LORD, is the greatness and the power and the glory and the majesty and the splendour, for everything in heaven and earth is yours. Yours, LORD, is the kingdom; you are exalted as head over all. Wealth and honour come from you; you are the ruler of all things. In your hands are strength and power to exalt and give strength to all. Now, our God, we give you thanks, and praise your glorious name" 1 Chronicles 29:10-13 NIV

> "You are worthy, our Lord and God, to receive glory and honour and power, for you created all things, and by your will they were created and have their being." Revelation 4:12 NIV

Never Alone

You are never abandoned, so don't give up
Just call out; find strength in a weakness cup
Look to God's heroes so strong from the past
By faith, they moved mountains and stood till the last

Don't think it is an easy road, following our Lord
Temptation surrounds us; we need God's holy sword
His sword deflects evil attacks from the foe
Imbued with His strength, to the world we show

In tiredness and emptiness, pray "God, make it right"
Breath in His Spirit and believe in His might
The cycles of life in constant ebb and bloom
Look beyond illness and self to transform the gloom

Some struggles in life can seem hard and long
But joy in God's Spirit can still inspire song
A song will replenish a tired empty soul
Refresh, renew, give God full control

Trusting by faith will grow courage and bind
Your fragile body, your heart, soul, and mind
To the One who loves you, be faithful and true
You are never alone; He's here for you.

God Is Everywhere

> I look behind me you're there, then up ahead and you're
> there too—your reassuring presence, coming and going.
> Psalm 139:5, The Message

Everywhere you are, God is. God is there in all the directions you take, no matter which way you choose to go. God is there in all the conditions of life, whatever their nature or intensity. God, who loves you enough to make you as special as you are, does not leave you alone at any time. God is at your side day after day and step by step.

In fact, when you find a place where you can be alone with God, God will pour out His blessings upon you. You can hear God speak to you in such a quiet, private place. There you can experience the holy presence of God.

Early in His life, Jesus formed the habit of frequently going away into the hills for quiet prayer to His Father. He went somewhere still and private. He would seek a quiet place for prayer, contemplation, and meditation. Create in your environment and within your heart a sanctuary for your soul to connect with the presence of God.

> For I am convinced that neither death nor life, neither
> angels or demons, neither the present or the future, nor
> any powers, neither height or depth, nor anything else in
> creation, will be able to separate us from the love of God
> that is in Christ Jesus our Lord. Romans 8:38–39, NIV

With these powerful promises, how can we doubt that God is always with us? Even though we may allow our human feelings of sadness to overwhelm us sometimes, He hears our call and will never leave or forsake us.

> When you lie down, you will not be afraid; when you lie
> down, your sleep will be sweet. Have no fear of sudden
> disaster or of the ruin that overtakes the wicked, for the
> Lord will be at your side and will keep your foot from
> being snared. Proverbs 3:24-26, NIV

One Day at a Time

My heart goes out to the ones who sit
With their blanket of loneliness and despair
With no one giving a care
Life can be cold like a lake, frozen and hard
Companionship, warmth, love,
all happiness barred

The warmth of a touch breaks
through the cold
To breathe, bring a smile, pierce the mould
The depth of love can set us free
And give us a smile for the universe to see

The flowers and seeds survive and remain
To grow again in the harsh domain
The fruit and fragrance of life don't last
Every night they're put in the past

With the dawn of each new day
It's another chance to find a better way
To break through the ice
To melt resentment, anger, and strife

For one day at a time flies by so fast
There is no yesterday, for it has passed
So, live each day and grow in trust
For one day, you too will be dust

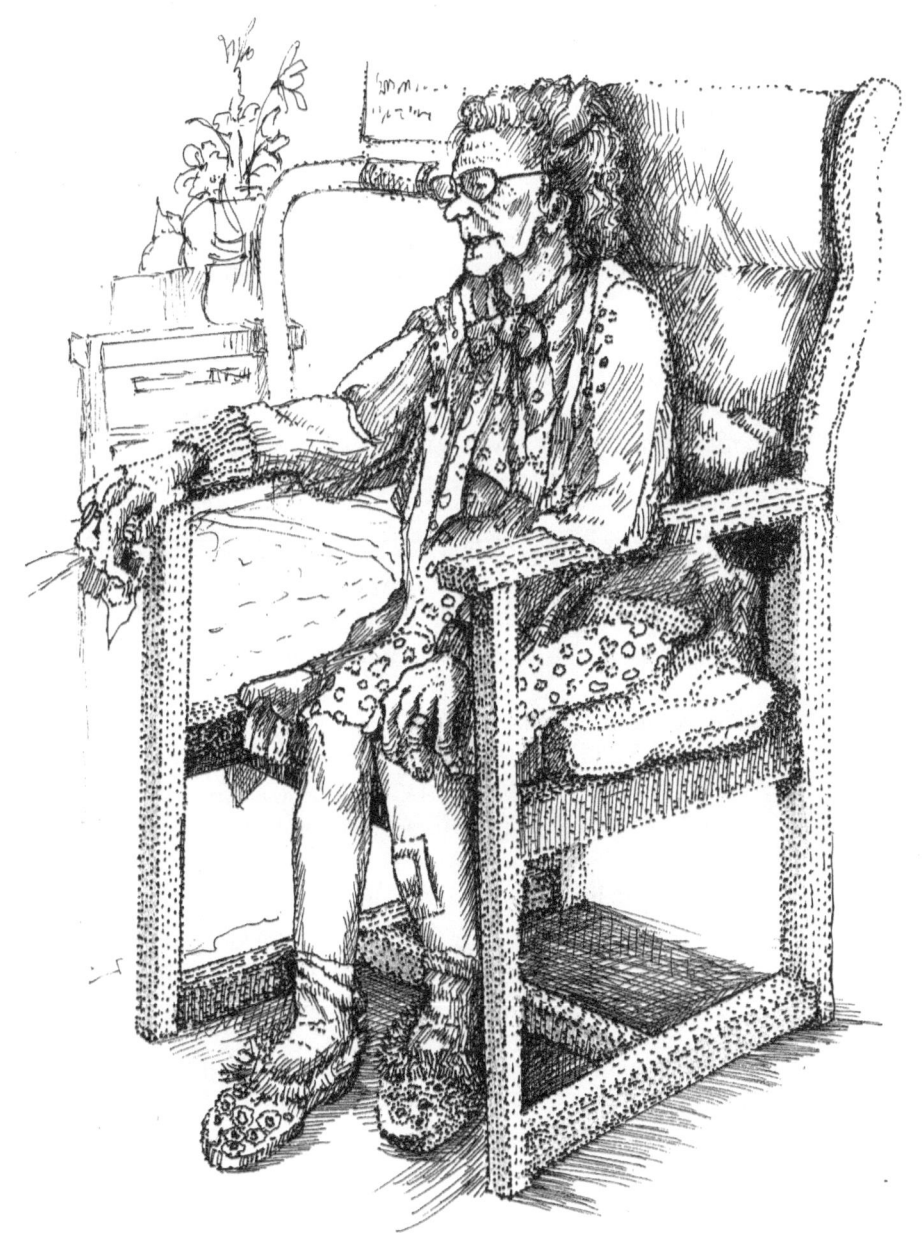

The Lonely Man

The man was now old, with wrinkled skin, hair thinning and grey
He stared out the window, wondering, did he waste his life away?
The days of his youth he remembered well, of vitality, strong
Lungs expanded, full of air, could pump out any song

Feeble now, he could hardly get out of the chair
His life restricted, with little joy, crowned solely by despair
So many years he perceived washed beneath his bridge
But how many, he wondered, did he really live?

The money he'd made won't keep him warm
Maybe build a house to weather the storm
The empire he'd sacrificed all love to make
Money, the only God to which he could relate

Now where do his children and grandchildren live?
He has so much stored-up love to share and give
Wondering if they are happy, their lives now a mystery
He now wished he knew their personal history

All the time he has wasted, he will never get back
His life is so much sadder for the love it lacks
The lack of arms to hug him or help him along
Grandkids to hear stories or share his loved songs

With an empty heart, grieving for what he's lost
He just didn't understand what moneymaking would cost
Of knowing that when his time on earth is done
In his solitary space, he will be the only one.

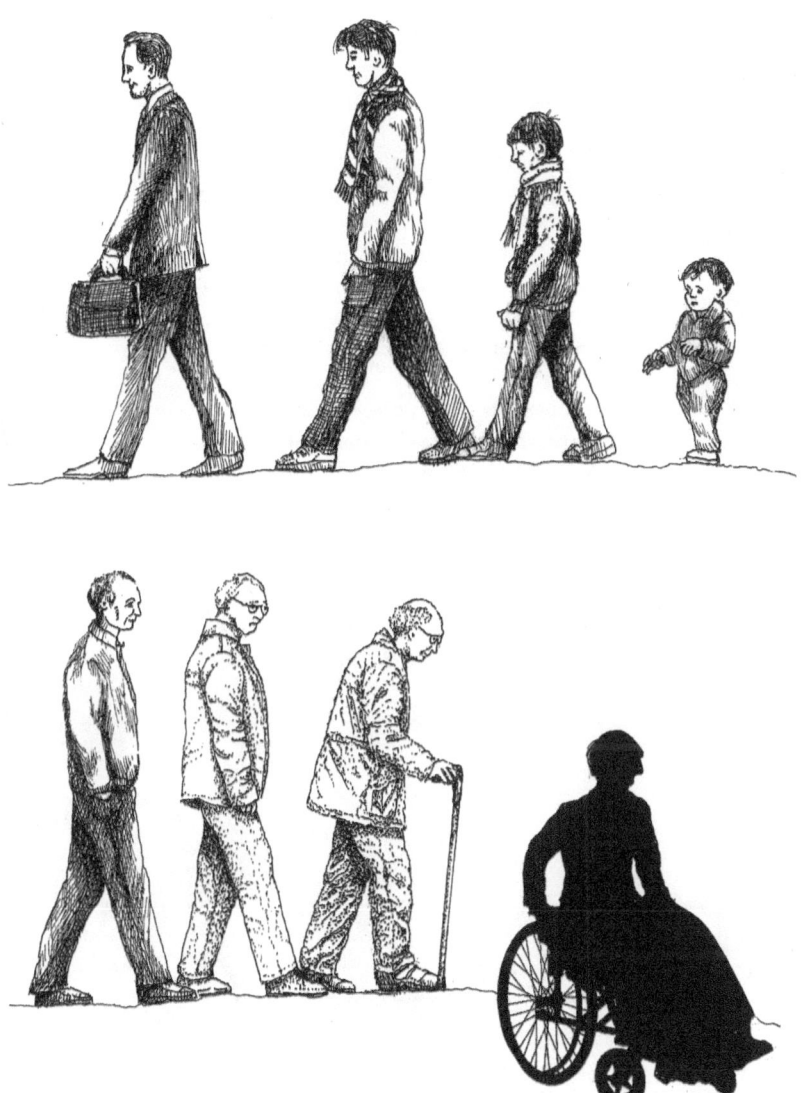

The Brave Face

The brave face is just a mask to hide from all those near
The loneliness, isolation, illness, pain, and fear
We all have assorted styles of masks for protection, it is true
Few choose to reveal the truth of it; perhaps that's you

Torn emotions swirl, hidden behind a mask
Living behind reality, emotions so vast
We show masked faces, so happy and strong
I'm not that different; I want to belong

My life is short and moving fast
I want to leave a good impression that will last
I want to be brave and journey calmly along
Behind my mask every day, perform a new song

Sometimes, my face is tinged with lonely tears
I know the Lord listens and eases my fears
He's done it before with profound peace so deep
His healing grace has restored rest and sleep

My eyes now twinkle and glow with Your might
For You are within, shedding an everlasting light
Spreading vitality, no mask needed now
You are my Lord; my faith is my vow.

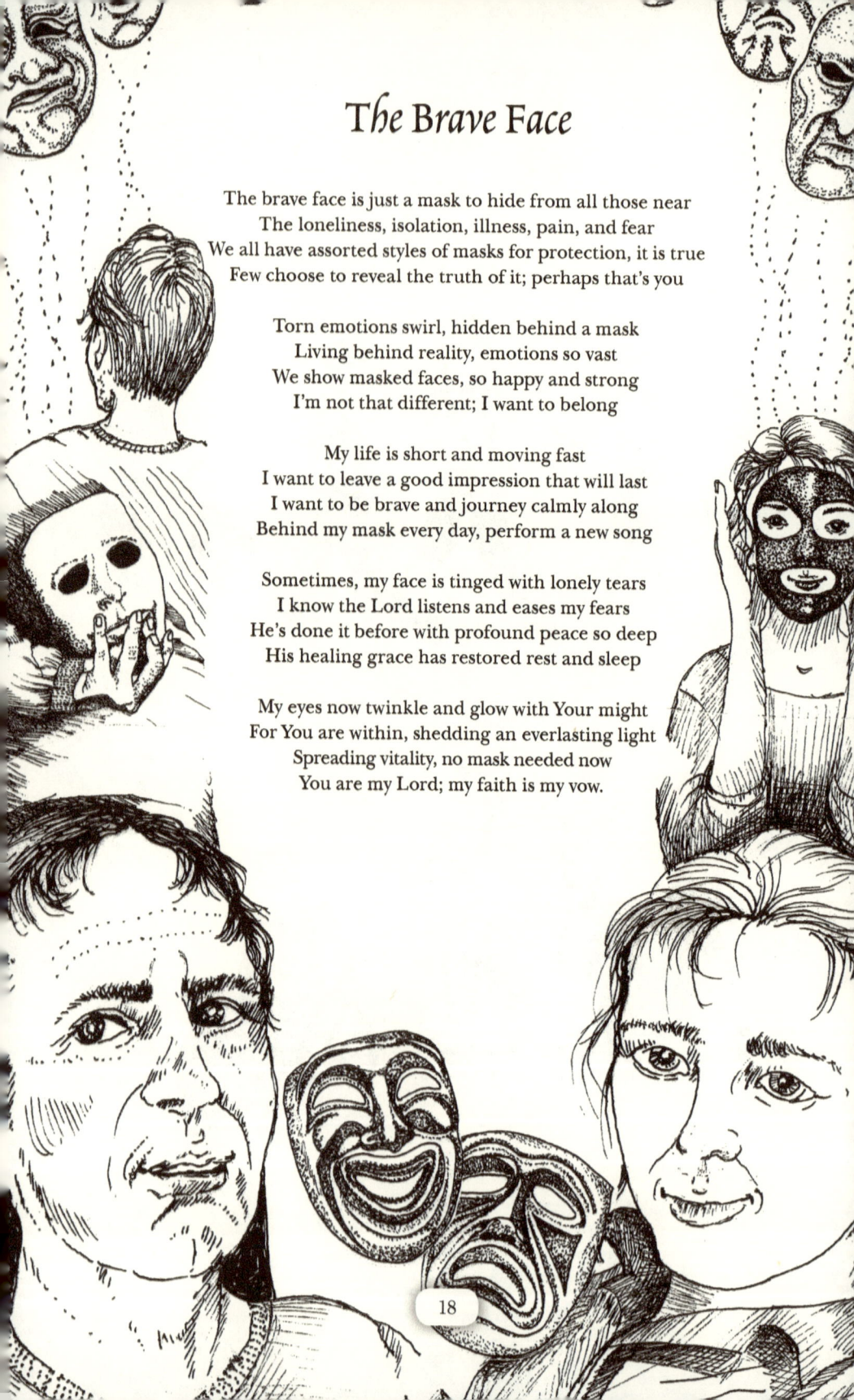

Masks Off

> The LORD told him, 'Samuel, don't think Eliab is the one just because he's tall and handsome . . . People judge others by what they look like, but I judge people by what is in their hearts.'
> 1 Samuel 16:7, CEV

At the Mardi Gras Museum in New Orleans, a large glass case holds various masks used in past carnival celebrations over a time span of hundreds of years. A printed legend propped inside the case called the Power of the Mask offers this explanation: 'A new face and different attire allows a masker to transcend everyday life and construct a new self, an altered psyche.'

God invites you to do just the opposite. He invites you to take off your masks, both the public and private ones. He wants to see you as you are. He wants you to see yourself as you are.

There need be no hiding in the presence of God, for you can be real with Him all the time.

> "Teach me your way, LORD, that I may rely on your faithfulness; give me an undivided heart, that I may fear your name. I will praise you, Lord my God, with all my heart; I will glorify your name forever. For great is your love toward me; you have delivered me from the depths, from the realm of the dead." Psalm 86:11-13, NIV

> "Rejoice in the Lord always. I will say it again: Rejoice! Let your gentleness be evident to all. The Lord is near. Do not be anxious about anything, but in every situation, by prayer and petition, with thanksgiving, present your requests to God. And the peace of God, which transcends all understanding, will guard your hearts and your minds in Christ Jesus. Finally, brothers and sisters, whatever is true, whatever is noble, whatever is right, whatever is pure, whatever is lovely, whatever is admirable—if anything is excellent or praiseworthy—think about such things. Whatever you have learned or received or heard from me or seen in me—put it into practice. And the God of peace will be with you." Philippians 4:4-9, NIV

> "God is our refuge and strength, an ever-present help in trouble. Therefore, we will not fear, though the earth gives way and the mountains fall into the heart of the sea, though its waters roar and foam and the mountains quake with their surging. There is a river whose streams make glad the city of God, the holy place where the Most High dwells." Psalm 46:1-4, NIV

The Gift

Illness is the cross I bear
Regardless, I'll follow my Lord everywhere
He's my shepherd; it's always true
He guides my way and gets me through

His faith and love are gifted to me
All who seek and ask, receive, you'll see
God's big love can cover us all
He cares so deeply when you answer His call

Then when our life is done and over
The tears, the laughter, and rolling in clover
To Him, we go, and by faith, it's true
This gift is open to all who choose.

What God's Love Means

God loves us so much that He rejoices over us singing with loud rejoicing over us with gladness

"The LORD your God is in your midst, a mighty one who will save; he will rejoice over you with gladness; he will quiet you by his love; he will exult over you with loud singing" Zephaniah 3:17 NIV

"In this the love of God was made manifest among us, that God sent his only Son into the world, so that we might live through him. In this is love, not that we have loved God but that he loved us and sent his Son to be the propitiation for our sins. Beloved, if God so loved us, we also ought to love one another" 1 John 4:9-11 NIV

Nothing can bring you greater joy than the conviction that God loves you. Regardless of what is happening in your life, don't lose sight of the truth. Pray it into your mind and heart every day.

"God who is rich in mercy, out of the great love with which He loved us even when we were dead through our sins, made us alive together with Christ". Ephesians 2:4-5 NIV

Think about what it means for God to love you. Think about God in heaven loving you enough to make you the unique and wonderful person you are. Think about God coming to earth as Jesus Christ, so He could get close enough to love you even more. Think about God loving you to such a degree that He walks with you every step you take in life. God loves us so much that He rejoices over us singing with loud rejoicing over us with gladness

The foundation of faith is God's love for you. God's love for you always comes first.

"When I am in distress, I call to you, because you answer me." Psalm 86:7 NIV

Once you have taken Jesus into your heart, and fully allow His love to fill the void that worldly things could never satisfy, then you will truly know the love of God. Gently and quietly filling up your heart and imbuing your spirit with strength.

The Fountain of Life

Waters that run still and deep
Fluid motion all through my soul does seep

Heart of the Spirit drawing near
Holds me close and defeats the fear

When God protects, none can touch
For God alone produces a fearless trust

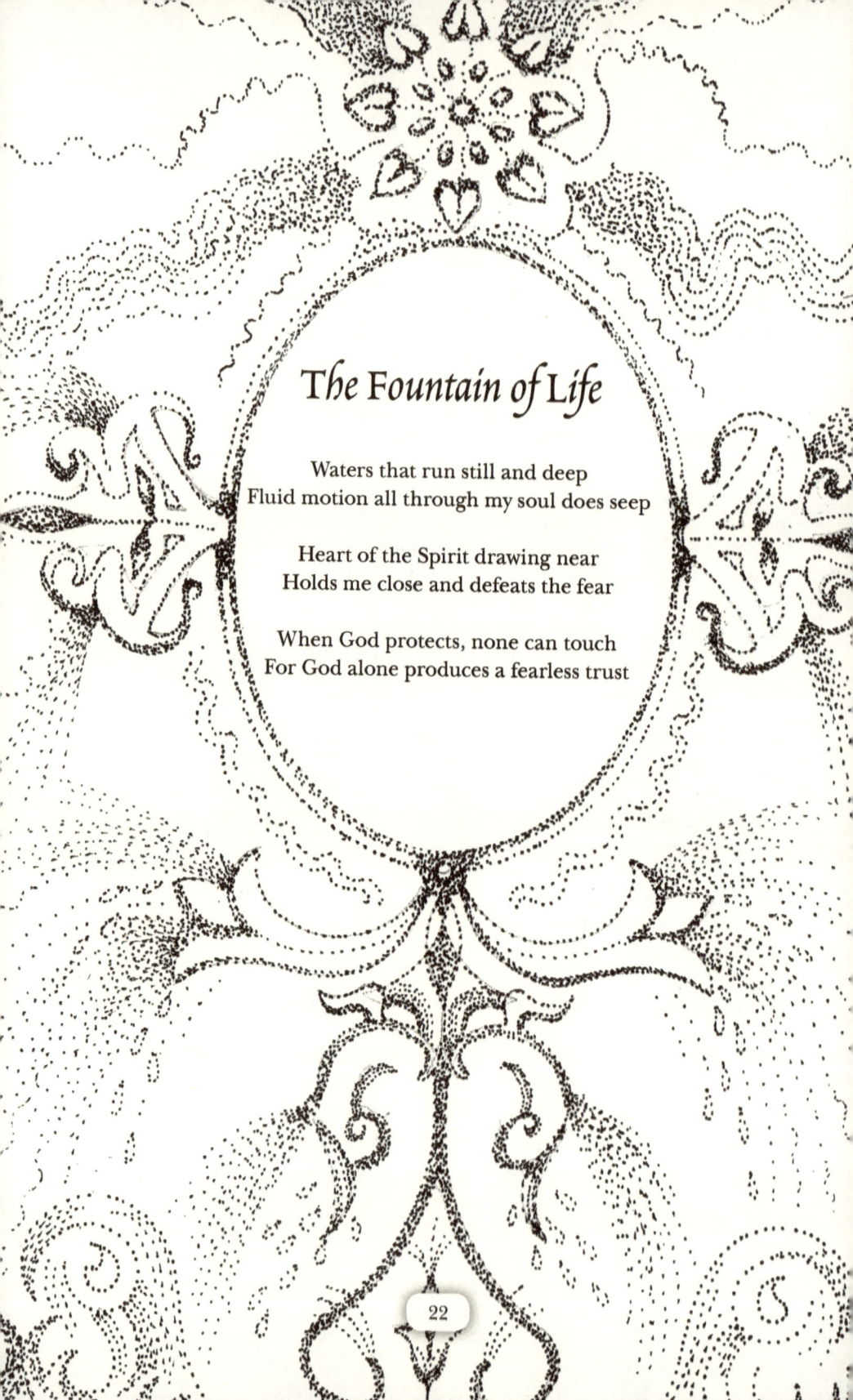

Everlasting Streams

> For I will pour water on the thirsty land,
> and streams on the dry ground;
> I will pour out my Spirit on your offspring,
> and my blessing on your descendants.
> They will spring up like grass in a meadow,
> like poplar trees by flowing streams.
> Some will say, I belong to the LORD;
> others will call themselves by the name of Jacob;
> still others will write on their hand, The LORD'S,
> and will take the name Israel. Isaiah 44:3–5

I personally love to claim this promise in the book of Isaiah. I find it comforting that my God will water and protect my children, grandchildren, and everyone in my family to come. I know that all good blessings come from the Lord our God.

God is continually sending His Holy Spirit to soothe, guide, and refresh us.

For those who belong to and rely on God are continually watered to bring new growth, understanding, and peace then to let this wonderful refreshment from our Lord flow on to others.

> But let justice roll on like a river, righteousness like a never-failing stream. Amos 5:24

The Whisper of My Spirit

Oh, how I want to hold you so lovingly to my breast
My yearning heart calls out to you and has no peace or rest
The whisper of my Spirit tapping gently on your soul
Surrender, remove deceptions veil,
and release your self- control

The cards and crystal readings, the seeking of the seers
Those lures of false prophecy, deceiving you for years.
Has this brought you closer to the true love pure, Divine?
A knowing in heart and soul that there's a true love to find

A new glow in your heart, bright as summers day
Healing grace in bone and sinew, now takes the pain away
Embrace love unconditional, of all pervasive power
To the deepest, darkest fear, love prevails now hour by hour

The world is full of tinsel, glitz and shallow dark delights
Look to Me for guidance, now new butterfly take flight
Come cleansed, I call you now in the deepness of your heart
Come to me, new born, spirit flesh now healed in every part

Ascribe Glory to the LORD

Listen to God's voice. His Spirit calls to you!

> Ascribe Glory to the LORD, O mighty ones,
> Ascribe Glory to the LORD glory and strength.
> Ascribe Glory to the LORD the glory due His name;
> Worship the LORD in the splendour of His holiness.
>
> The voice of the LORD is over the waters;
> The God of glory thunders,
> The LORD thunders over the mighty waters.
> The voice of the LORD is powerful;
> The voice of the LORD is majestic. Psalm 29:1-4, NIV

Turn to Truth's Light

How dark is the conviction of the soul to sin?
Like a black tie that chains us from within.
The evil of sin can pervade anyone,
Leaves empty bleakness without God's only Son.

The path of false teaching seems so very clear,
But the burden of sin is alive and well there.
In the world of deception's enticing delights,
False seers and guides say their ways are right.

Use these rocks, special crystals, they say,
To give you special powers and make you a star.
Be full of yourself and become a god.
Take your own path; ignore wisdom well-trod.

The attractive promises that are made to you
Can never redeem you, for they are not true.
Oh, the theatre of grandeur,
world's heady delights!
They will whisper and draw you into their sights.

You have only one life to make it right.
So seek and search with all your might.
The Creator God is universally true
Just ask, He'll reveal the true light to you.

The way of the true light is muddied by some
To lead us astray from God's dear Son.
He alone is the living proof, the
guide, and the light,
His Holy Spirit's power to keep you in His might.

The Holy Spirit within us houses God's room.
His grace is sufficient to cleanse away any gloom.
Give welcome to God; He'll blast through the dark.
He'll fill and heal damaged depths in your heart.

Through Him, you'll discern between
the false and the true.
Jesus's name above all names,
love filling you through.
All yearn to unburden, run life's race and win.
Seek ye first God's kingdom and be freed from sin.

See the Light

Jesus once again addressed them: 'I am the world's Light. No one who follows Me stumbles around in the darkness. I provide plenty of light to live in.' John 8:12, The Message

The people who walked in darkness have seen a great light. For those who lived in the land of deep shadows—light! Sunbursts of light! Isaiah 9:2, The Message

See to it that no one takes you captive through hollow and deceptive philosophy, which depends on human tradition and the elemental spiritual forces of this world rather than on Christ. For in Christ all the fullness of the Deity lives in bodily form. Colossians 2:8-9, NIV

At that time if anyone says to you, 'Look, here is the Messiah!' or, 'There he is!' do not believe it. For false messiahs and false prophets will appear and perform great signs and wonders to deceive, if possible, even the elect. Matthew 24:23-24, NIV

A lit candle in a church is a symbol for the light of God's presence. Light is God's nature. That is why in the Jewish tabernacle, a perpetual lamp burned, a light that never went out. It was there to remind the people of the ever-present light of God.

Do not let anyone who delights in false humility and the worship of angels disqualify you. Such a person also goes into detail about what they have seen; they are puffed up with idle notions by their unspiritual mind. Colossians 2:18, NIV

Blessed are those who have learned to acclaim you, who walk in the light of your presence, LORD. Psalm 89:15, NIV

This is the message we have heard from him and declare to you: God is light; in him there is no darkness at all. 1 John 1:5, NIV

The sun will no more be your light by day, nor will the brightness of the moon shine on you, for the LORD will be your everlasting light, and your God will be your glory. Isaiah 60:19, NIV

Nothing eliminates the darkness of the world like the light of God. Like the light of God, it is a fire that burns in your heart and won't go out even in dark and tough times. As you draw close to God, you will experience divine light upon your path. When that light comes, follow it.

The Rudderless Ship

The rudder on a ship is very small
But misuse will make a mighty ship fall
So like us and our bodies within
The tongue is the rudder, small and slim

Oh, the havoc this little part can bring
The lies and deception that can sting
Bring even a mighty warrior to his knees
Buckled down until all confidence flees

The slurs to character stabbing the heart
The wounds of these words
will never depart
So think with your mind and take control
Of your tongue and the damage it can hold.

Taming the Tongue

A Wholesome tongue is a tree of life. Proverbs 15:4, NIV

When we put bits into the mouths of horses to make them obey us, we can turn the whole animal. Or take ships as an example. Although they are so large and are driven by fierce winds, they are steered by a very small rudder wherever the pilot wants to go. Likewise, the tongue is a small part of the body, but it makes great boasts. Consider what a great forest is set on fire by a small spark. The tongue also is a fire, a world of evil among the parts of the body. It corrupts the whole body, sets the whole course of one's life on fire, and is itself set on fire by hell. All kinds of animals, birds, reptiles and sea creatures are being tamed and have been tamed by mankind, but no human being can tame the tongue. It is a restless evil, full of deadly poison. With the tongue we praise our LORD and Father, and with it we curse human beings, who have been made in God's likeness. Out of the same mouth come praise and cursing. My brothers and sisters, this should not be. Can both fresh water and salt water flow from the same spring? My brothers and sisters, can a fig tree bear an olive, or a grapevine bear a fig? Neither can a salt spring produce fresh water. James 3:3-12, NIV

Life and death are in the power of the tongue. Proverbs 18:21, NSV

Keep your tongue from evil. Psalm 34:13, NSV

Set a guard over my mouth, LORD; keep watch over the door of my lips. Psalm 141:3, NIV

He who goes about as a talebearer reveals secrets; therefore, do not associate with one who flatters with him lips. Proverbs 20:19, NIV

Gossip or a nasty word about or towards another can never be taken back. Once the words have been said the damage is done. Think about this, God hears all you say and sees what you do. It's recorded in the Book of Life. The tongue though small can encourage and build or equally devastate and destroy. Think before you speak. Pray that God builds within you a generous and loving heart that encourages positive speech and actions as a natural outcome of loving the Lord your God with all your heart, mind, spirit and loving others as yourself

> For, 'Whoever would love life and see good days must keep their tongue from evil and their lips from deceitful speech. They must turn from evil and do good; they must seek peace and pursue it. all your heart, mind and spirit and loving others as yourself.' 1 Peter 3:10-11 NIV

Temptation

Temptation comes in many forms, always to lure our soul
Calling the sinful nature that strives to take control
Whispering, deceitful, and boastful untruths
The sin corrupting and taking strong roots

Of course, it seems the easy way to turn a blind eye
To seek pleasures and riches and never wonder why
The world is starving for love and simple comfort
The sin takes control to give it up is a last resort

How do we break the chain of temptation?
By giving our all to Christ, pray with contemplation
For only then can the Holy Spirit come through
To comfort, love, and bring out the best in you

The armour of God we need to wear for full protection
For only then can we avoid sin's deceitful detection
As of course, human we are, sometimes we will stumble
But return to the Lord, loving, sincere, and humble

Jesus walked the path of temptation too
When your weak, He will give His strength to you
Just ask when you're feeling it's all too much
He died for you; He will come with a gentle touch

From the LORD Comes Deliverance

Have no doubt that the devil *will* most certainly tempt us all. He knows his time is short, and he wants as many as possible to lose eternal salvation.

> Be self-controlled and alert, your enemy the devil prowls around like a roaring loin looking for someone to devour. 1 Peter 5:8, NIV

The devil will attack families, finances, work, and the church. He will know, by studying you, where your weakest areas are, and in every part of our life, He will tempt us, especially when we decide to follow our Shepherd, Jesus. But don't fear the evil one. When you are tempted, you have a rescuer.

> Rescue me from my enemies, Oh LORD, for I hide myself in you. Teach me to do your will for you are my God, may Your Good Spirit lead me on level ground. Psalm 143:9–10, NIV

> He rescues, and He saves; He performs signs and wonders in the heavens and on the earth. He has rescued Daniel from the power of the lions. Daniel 6:27, NIV

> From the LORD comes deliverance, may Your blessing be upon Your people. Psalm 3:8, NIV

> The LORD is my rock, my fortress and my deliverer, my God is my rock, in whom I take refuge. He is my shield and the horn of my salvation, my stronghold. Psalm 18:2, NIV

> For he will deliver the needy who cry out, the afflicted who have on one to help. He will take pity on the weak and the needy and save the needy from death. He will rescue them from oppression and violence, for precious is their blood in His sight. Psalm 72:12-14, NIV

We must know our need and CRY out for help. If we stubbornly choose to remain independent of God, then He can't help us. Stick close to Jesus. He is our Shepherd and knows the safest way.

> Trust in The LORD with all your heart, and lean not on your own understanding, in all your ways acknowledge Him and He will you're your paths straight. Proverbs 3:5-6, NIV

> I will put my trust in Him. Hebrews 2:13, NIV

Money

If I had so much money to fill the earth
I'd build houses and save
lives to prove its worth
The money we have will surely go
When we die, it stays here below!

For gold and jewellery are the devil's tools
That can excite the greed of many fools
Money can cause all kinds of grief
Jealousy, envy, there's just no release

The want of wealth can send you mad
Lose your truth and the best friends you had
Better to be kind and give with love
To lead a life led by God above

Stay clear and focused on the day
And lead and give in every way
For there's only one life to live
So find peace and happiness to give

Money can't buy the things of worth
The joy of vision and new birth
Hearing the words 'I love you'
And richness of love to fill you through

For love is the answer, not money that binds
To leave the hurt and sorrow behind
All you need is here now, within your soul
God's love, not money, will make you whole

The Want of Money

Money was first mentioned in the scriptures in Genesis 17:12, so the issues relating to money have been around for thousands of years.

King Solomon has some wisdom regarding money for us:

> Whoever loves money never has money enough; whoever loves wealth is never satisfied with his income. This too is meaningless. As goods increase so do those who consume them, and what benefit are they to the owner except to feast his eyes on them. Ecclesiastes 5:10–11, NIV

Other Bible prophets make it very clear how money will not save anyone.

> They will throw their silver into the streets, and their gold will be an unclean thing, their silver and gold will not be able to save them in the day of The Lord's wrath. Ezekiel 7:19-20, NIV

There are a lot of references to money in the New Testament, and very wise words they are.

> Keep your lives free from the love of money and be content with what you have, because God has said 'I will never leave you; never forsake you.' Hebrews 13:5, NIV

> For the love of money is the root of all kinds of evil. Some people eager for money have wandered from the faith and pierced themselves with many griefs. 1 Timothy 6:10, NIV

> Now the overseer must be above reproach, the husband of but one wife, temperate, self-controlled, respectable, hospitable, able to teach, not given to drunkenness, not violent but gentle, not quarrelsome, not a lover of money. 1 Timothy 3:2–3, NIV

> Be shepherds of God's flock that is under your care, serving as overseers—not because you must, but because you are willing, as God wants you to be, not greedy for money but eager to serve. 1 Peter 5:2, NIV

The Pain of Separation

The separation and isolation of my pain
Makes me weep again and again
I want to shine like the morning sun
And bring glory and praise to God's only Son

I've redemption and healing from my Lord
Cried heartfelt prayers and read His Word
Although the pain of separation is great
To my soul, His Love and peace do relate

His amazing love and kindness
Come to remove my blindness
But there will be a stone hanging around my heart
Until, dear Lord, I am with You, never to depart

This world of money, fame, and power
Becomes as nothing, a crumbling tower
Stuck together with a greedy glue
All I desire, Lord, is to be close to You

So through my life I live for You
Show me, tell me what to do
To bring Your kingdom of love to all
Then none again will ever fall

The beauty of nature is astounding to see
However, Jesus is the most wonderful to me
I am here to follow my precious Lord
And spread His love that all can afford

I wish now that, Jesus, You were here
My impatience washes over me
Come soon, dear Saviour, to make me sound
Released from pain; confident, I'm homeward bound

Hold Onto God

> The righteous cry out, and the LORD hears, and delivers them out of all their troubles. The LORD is near to those who have a broken heart and saves such as have a contrite spirit. Psalm 34:17–18, NKJV

There is a time to be broken down, a time that we should come to God in proper sorrow. The Hebrew word translated as 'contrite' can mean 'crushed'. God is near those whose selfish, prideful mind has been broken down, and He saves those whose spirit is crushed.

> We are hard-pressed on every side, yet not crushed; we are perplexed, but not in despair; persecuted, but not forsaken; struck down, but not destroyed. 2 Corinthians 4:8–9, NIV

In the following years after Christ's death, the early followers were heavily persecuted. They clung fast to their faith and the promises of complete healing to come.

> So, we may boldly say: 'The LORD is my helper; I will not fear. What can man do to me?' Hebrews 13:6, NIV

> 'Hear my cry, O God; attend unto my prayer. From the end of the earth will I cry unto you, when my heart is overwhelmed: lead me to the rock that is higher than I.' Psalm 61:1–2, NKJV

The psalmist David felt overwhelmed about something that happened in his life, but he still celebrated God as his high and secure rock. David used many images to paint a picture of how God protected him in the midst of trouble and kept him safe when danger came near.

So when you feel at the end of your rope, hang on to the knot of security and steadfastness that God has tied there.

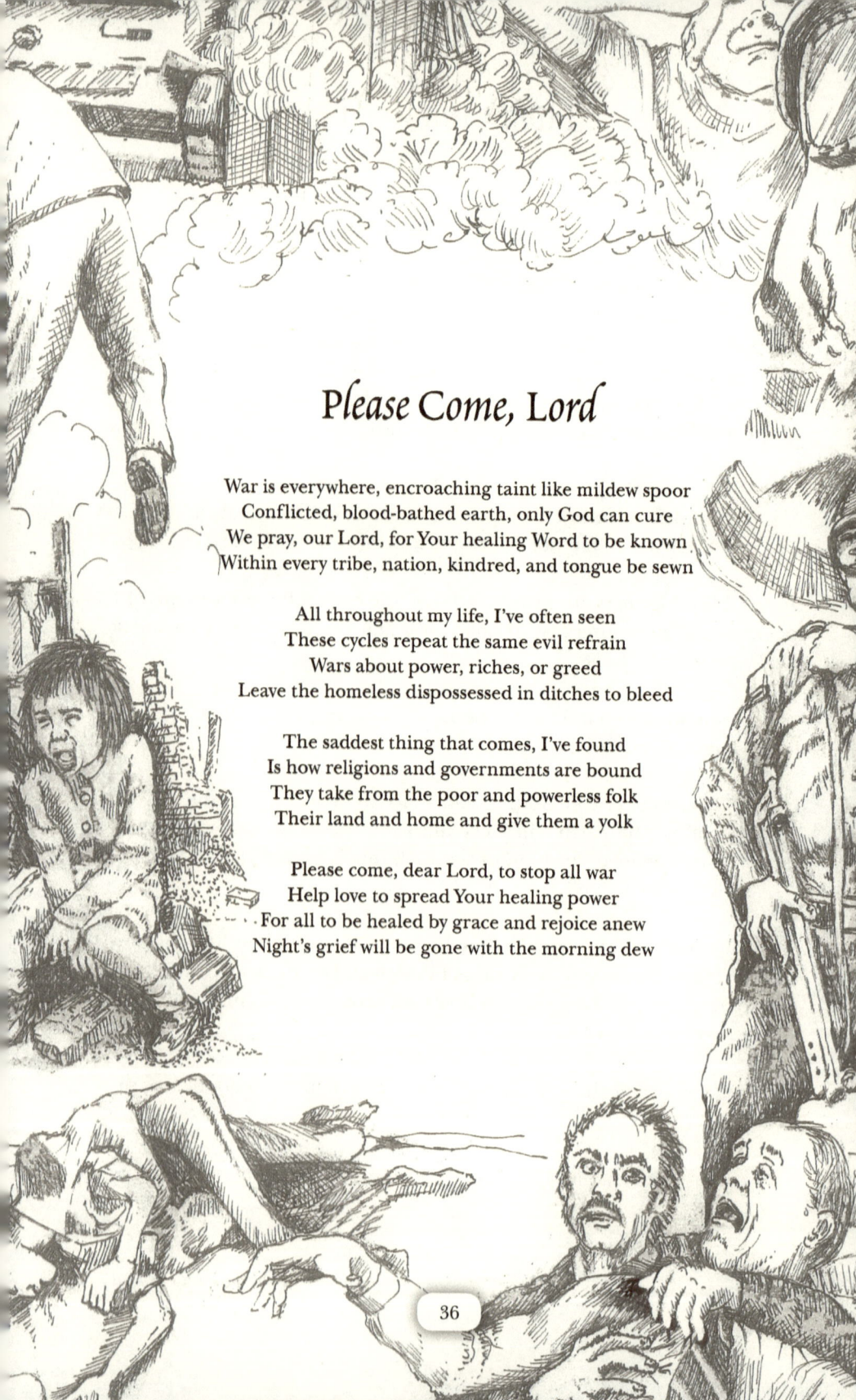

Please Come, Lord

War is everywhere, encroaching taint like mildew spoor
Conflicted, blood-bathed earth, only God can cure
We pray, our Lord, for Your healing Word to be known
Within every tribe, nation, kindred, and tongue be sewn

All throughout my life, I've often seen
These cycles repeat the same evil refrain
Wars about power, riches, or greed
Leave the homeless dispossessed in ditches to bleed

The saddest thing that comes, I've found
Is how religions and governments are bound
They take from the poor and powerless folk
Their land and home and give them a yolk

Please come, dear Lord, to stop all war
Help love to spread Your healing power
For all to be healed by grace and rejoice anew
Night's grief will be gone with the morning dew

God Will Rescue Us

God has promised to rescue us not only from wartime situations, but in every aspect of our lives, He brings the sunshine in the morning.

Some of the most amazing rescues I can think of are when Daniel was rescued from the lion's den (please read Daniel 6:20) and when his companions, Shadrach, Meshach, and Abednego, were saved from a burning furnace. Not their skin, hair, or anywhere on them showed any sign of fire or singeing; even their clothes did not smell.

The fire was made seven times hotter than usual; it was so hot that the guards throwing them into the fire fell dead before they threw them in; that is why Daniel's friends fell into the fire.

> Shadrach, Meshach and Abednego replied to him, 'King Nebuchadnezzar, we do not need to defend ourselves before you in this matter. If we are thrown into the blazing furnace, the God we serve is able to deliver us from it, and he will deliver us from Your Majesty's hand. But even if he does not, we want you to know, Your Majesty, that we will not serve your gods or worship the image of gold you have set up.' Daniel 3:16–18, NIV

What amazing faith in the face of death. What assurance, devotion, and love.

Do you trust God with every demanding situation in your life? Do you have trouble letting go of all the difficult issues in life? Trust in God and give your difficulties to God. Through the power of the indwelling Spirit, you will receive the strength to keep on going, even into a blazing furnace.

These are dramatic stories of God's unfathomable power to deliver us. He also can deliver us from unhealthy habits, unkind thoughts, depression—the list go on.

There are, however, conditions. We need to ask and rely on Him alone and then believe He is able.

Be Strong

So many times, life choices can lead you astray
Be strong, patiently look for another way
There are so many choices, so many roads
Be careful; your choice may come with a load

Do we really take time to consider and wisely choose?
Or too quickly take chances, thinking there's nothing to lose
Take the easy road and do as others do
Bypass the best way; don't stick with the true

With your goal in mind, the plan all set
The wrong way can rob you and take your best
Be strong and don't take the easy road
because it may trap you and make you implode

Be strong, be true, and bless others with love
God will cherish your loyalty in heaven above
The world can be full of spite and remorse
Overlooks the narrow, where love is the source

Love to make us whole and give us a purpose
To dig deep, not just scratch the surface
Live, spread your gifts and love all around
Honour the Source, where this love is found

An honourable life is lived for others
Follow God's way, and with blessings be covered
None are without sin or perfect, it's true
Lies and deception can undermine all, even you

We are all vulnerable sometimes and can easily fall
Show compassion, don't judge, just follow God's call
Wrong judgements will always come back to you
So, be strong; be true in all you do

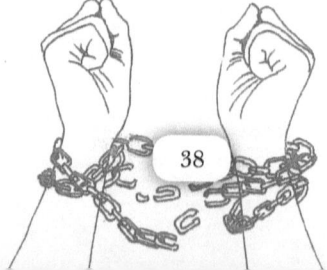

Spiritually Strong

There are so many choices in life, and there will be tough decisions to make.

> Do not be deceived: God cannot be mocked. A man reaps what he sows. Whoever sows to please their flesh, from the flesh will reap destruction; whoever sows to please the Spirit, from the Spirit will reap eternal life. Galatians 6:7-9, NIV

Not only that there could also be peer pressure to joint in the rest, and sometimes to be accepted we may make a bad choice. Concerning bad choices, my dad used to say, 'If they told you to jump in a fire, would you do it?'

Turn to the Lord for guidance. He will always give you free will to choose. Be careful. Remember to seek Him in silence to gain clarity and hear the still, quiet voice in our ears.

> Whether you turn to the right or to the left, your ears will hear a voice behind you, saying, 'This is the way; walk in it.' Isaiah 30:21, NIV

> Do not conform yourselves to the standards of this world but let God transform you inwardly by a complete change of your mind. Romans 12:2, GNT

Live life by the Spirit for a God filled love

> But the fruit of the Spirit is love, joy, peace, forbearance, kindness, goodness, faithfulness, gentleness and self-control. Against such things there is no law. Galatians 5:22–23, NIV

As one popular admonition phrases it, 'Live so the preacher won't have to lie at your funeral.'

Rise Up with Jesus

The struggles of this world
Grow and swell like tidal a wave
Carry all away into loneliness and pain
Scared we may be; rescue seems in vain

In this dark world, we have a Saviour
Jesus is a safe harbour, a delight to favour
With Christ, our shield, we have no fear
Though threat and danger are very near

When waves engulf a shaking heart
Swallowed under until nearly torn apart
Jesus will captain us through the storm
To still the waves and keep us warm

Seek the consolation of God's dear Son
Who shines a light on the path for everyone
Even in the darkest, coldest night
My soul clings to Him and His might

Love from Jesus encompasses me
Gently, softly, setting me free
Oh, how I wish the world would turn
To the love of Him and truly yearn

For when His love is held within
We are free from the bondage of sin
When smarting from Satan's deadly sting
Jesus comes to save, and a new life He brings

We sing of the joy of a life brand new
Promised to us by the One who is true
Through all the trouble, worry, and strife
He calms our soul and directs our life

Stand Tall with Faith in Your Heart

> Now faith is the confidence that what we hope for will actually happen; it gives us assurance about things we cannot see. Through their faith, the people in days of old earned a good reputation. Hebrews 11:1–2, NLT

When times are tough, just know that through faith in the unseen, you will be rewarded. The reward may not be something you enjoy in this life, but rather looking forward to our Lord Jesus's return, when He will give us healing and love like never known in this worldly existence. No pain or suffering even for the animals—how wonderful. No persecution.

> The wolf will live with the lamb, the leopard will lie down with the goat, the calf and the lion and the yearling together; and a little child will lead them. The cow will feed with the bear, their young will lie down together, and the lion will eat straw like the ox. The infant will play near the cobra's den, and the young child will put its hand into the viper's nest. They will neither harm nor destroy on all my holy mountain, for the earth will be filled with the knowledge of the LORD as the waters cover the sea. Isaiah 11:6-9, NIV

However, while we are here in this earthly existence, we will need to pursue this value that will strengthen us and fortify us in times of great need.

> The mind governed by the flesh is death, but the mind governed by the Spirit is life and peace. Romans 8:6 , NIV

> The Lord upholds all who fall and raises up all who are bowed down. The eyes of all look expectantly to You, And You give them their food in due season. You open Your Hand And satisfy the desire of every living thing. Psalm 145:14-16, NIV

Behold, He's Knocking at Your Door

Behold! He's knocking at your door
Choose to open, and you'll know for sure
His voice of love is calling to you
'Come, dine with Me to be reborn anew'

He has a table of the finest fare
With sincerity, humility, qualities so rare
He fills the hungry and lost with love
His touch is as gentle as a dove

The love He gives will satisfy
No need to question or wonder why
As His unconditional love and grace
Shines in your radiant face

Jesus stands knocking at your door,
Just open; He's been many times before
Just open your heart and your ears
He's been standing knocking for many years

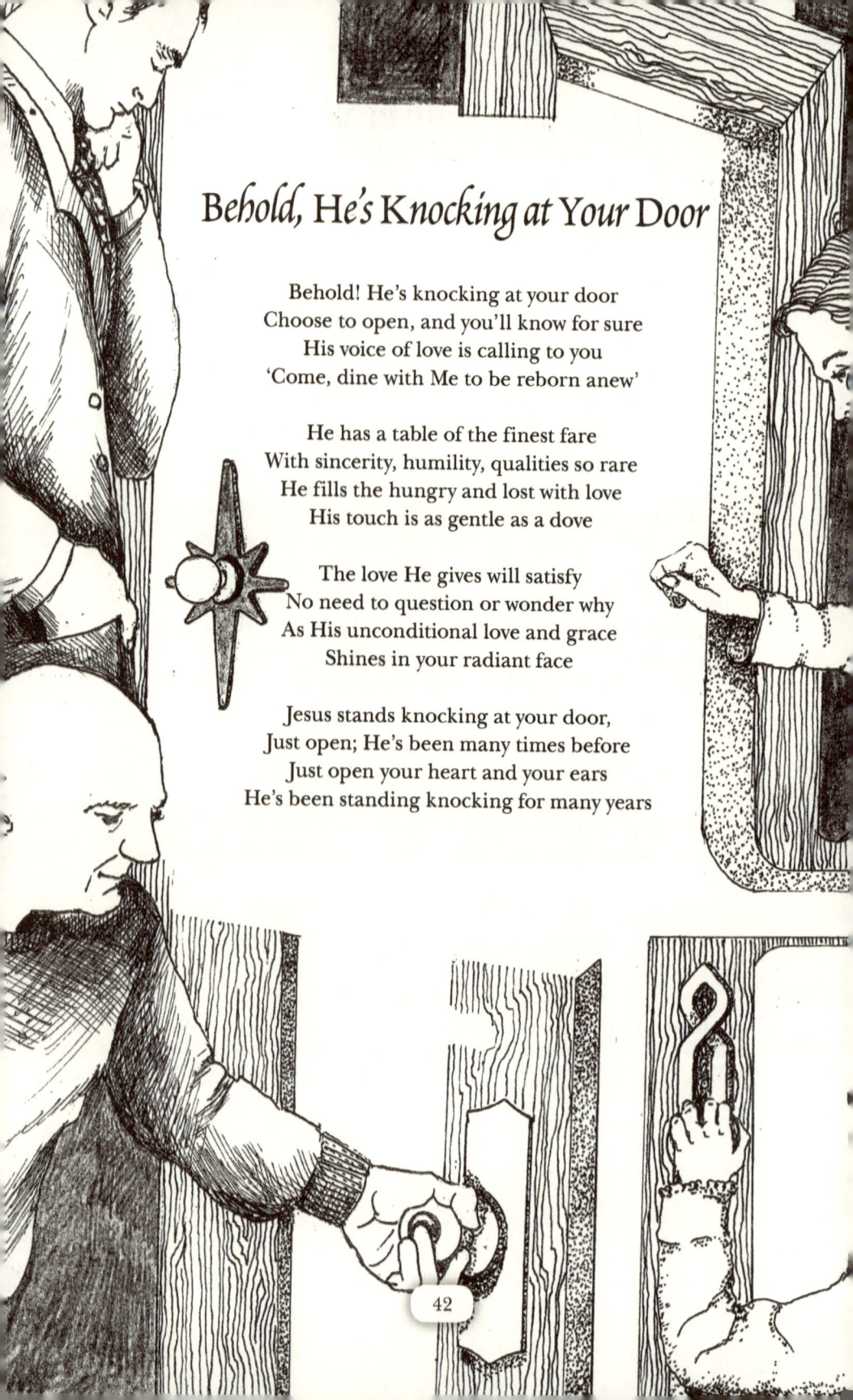

I Am the Door

> I assure you most solemnly I tell you, that I AM the Door for the sheep. John 10:7, NIV

As a carpenter and craftsman, Jesus understood the importance of doors. He knew that doors gave people access. In the construction of the usual wooden door, there are four panels separated by a long upright centreboard and a shorter horizontal board. These two boards form the pattern of a cross. This long-utilized plan for making doors came from a carpenters' guild in England in the Middle Ages. The artisans in that guild worked the sign of the cross into every door they made. It is no surprise that the motto of this carpenters' guild was the words Jesus spoke to the people in Jerusalem: 'I am the door.'

> Listen! I am standing at the door, knocking; if you hear my voice and open the door, I will come in to you and eat with you, and you with me. Revelation 3:20, NIV

Listen for the knock of opportunity on the door of life. God sends opportunity because he loves you and wants the best for you. You are His child, and He will provide you with occasions to do well. He has many wonderful places for you to be, and He will provide you with the means to get them. Open every door on which you hear a knock because behind each door is a fresh possibility. God knocks on the door of your heart to give you gifts of grace and joy.

> So, I say to you: Ask and it will be given to you; seek and you will find; knock and the door will be opened to you. For everyone who asks receives; the one who seeks finds; and to the one who knocks, the door will be opened. Luke 11:9–10, NIV

> Pray that God will open up to us a door for the word, so that we may speak forth the mystery of Christ. Colossians 4:3, NIV

The Armour of God

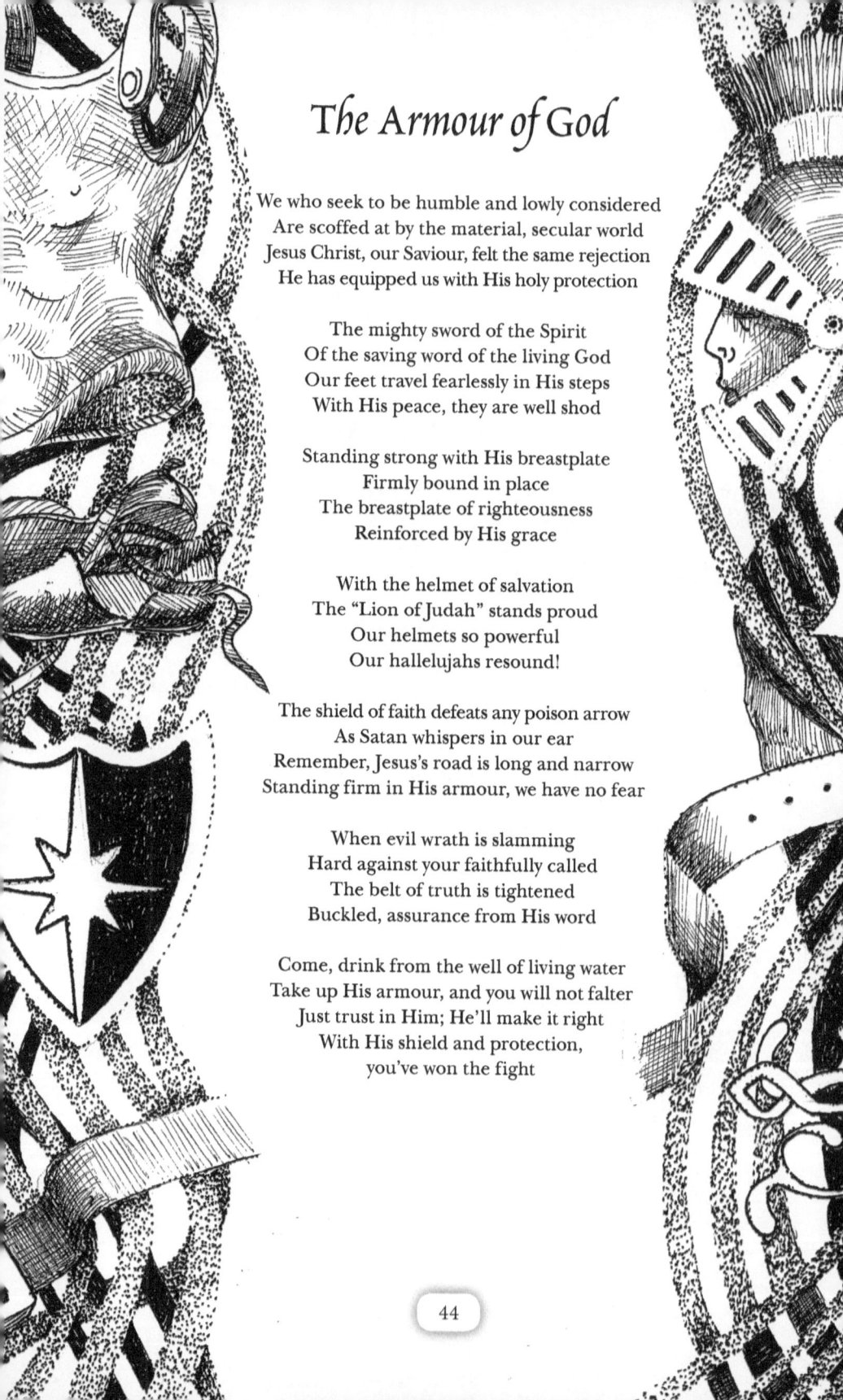

We who seek to be humble and lowly considered
Are scoffed at by the material, secular world
Jesus Christ, our Saviour, felt the same rejection
He has equipped us with His holy protection

The mighty sword of the Spirit
Of the saving word of the living God
Our feet travel fearlessly in His steps
With His peace, they are well shod

Standing strong with His breastplate
Firmly bound in place
The breastplate of righteousness
Reinforced by His grace

With the helmet of salvation
The "Lion of Judah" stands proud
Our helmets so powerful
Our hallelujahs resound!

The shield of faith defeats any poison arrow
As Satan whispers in our ear
Remember, Jesus's road is long and narrow
Standing firm in His armour, we have no fear

When evil wrath is slamming
Hard against your faithfully called
The belt of truth is tightened
Buckled, assurance from His word

Come, drink from the well of living water
Take up His armour, and you will not falter
Just trust in Him; He'll make it right
With His shield and protection,
you've won the fight

Spiritual Armour

Finally, be strong in the Lord and in his mighty power. Put on the full Armor of God, so that you can take your stand against the devil's schemes. For our struggle is not against flesh and blood, but against the rulers, against the authorities, against the powers of this dark world and against the spiritual forces of evil in the heavenly realms. Therefore, put on the full Armor of God, so that when the day of evil comes, you may be able to stand your ground, and after you have done everything, to stand.

Stand firm then, with the belt of truth buckled around your waist,

With the breastplate of righteousness in place,

With your feet fitted with the readiness that comes from the gospel of peace.

In addition to all this, take up the shield of faith, with which you can extinguish all the flaming arrows of the evil one.

Take the helmet of salvation and the sword of the Spirit, which is the word of God.

And pray in the Spirit on all occasions with all kinds of prayers and requests. Be alert and always keep on praying for all the Lord's people. Ephesians 6:10–18, NIV

Would you ever leave home half dressed? Of course not!

However, many of us forget to put on our spiritual clothing. Every day evil is arrayed against you, and it's important to be protected! With God's spiritual protection and authority, you can stand firmly against evil forces. Learn about your spiritual armour, and as you put on your clothes each day, also put on your armour and pick up your sword!

Don't Delay

I used to think friendship would last the test
Support and love, enduring the rest
My heart cries, 'Friends, where are you now?'
Come and sing with me; I'll show you how

Don't wait till you throw a flower on my grave
But rather give while you can, your soul to save
Be a friend with honesty shining through
So while you can be strong and true

When you're weeping with sadness and stop to say
Such a shame, she had to go that way!
The chance has passed to share laugher and jokes
With your mate, just one of the folks

Bring a smile and share a tear
Choose to be close and half the fear
So remember now, while you may
Don't let your loyal friends get away

Remember Others

Talk to God about other people. Talk to Him about who is physically sick and the form of sickness. Tell God who is under emotional stress and the cause of their anxiety. Tell God about the people you know who are lonely or others who are financially strung out, unable to take care of their families as they want to. Tell God who is experiencing grief, a shattered dream, or depression and who can't seem to get up off the floor. Physically assist them if they need it. Serve others. Be humble as Christ's example shows us. Deep compassion and empathy are demonstrated when we lift the names and conditions of others to God. Let God know that you deeply desire that He meet their greatest needs and ask that He help them in their time of trial.

Get in touch with the people you are praying for. Tell them you have appealed to our Heavenly Father to ease and comfort them, always praying in the faith and name of Jesus, who is our intercessor. Also offer help with domestic duties and the practical things, like transport and shopping.

> He is able to save forever those who draw near to God through Him, since He always lives to make intercession for them. Hebrews 7:25, NASB

> But love your enemies, do good to them, and lend to them without expecting to get anything back. Then your reward will be great, and you will be children of the Most High, because he is kind to the ungrateful and wicked. Be merciful, just as your Father is merciful. Luke 6:35–36, NIV

Now, every time I read this verse in Luke, I am reminded of my own inabilities to rise above demanding situations/people and just love them. I need God's transforming power working within me to even get close to achieving this level of love.

> If your enemy is hungry, give him food to eat; if he is thirsty, give him water to drink. In doing this, you will heap burning coals on his head, and the LORD will reward you. Proverbs 25:21–22, NIV

Don't Mourn for Me

Please don't mourn for me
I'm going where I want to be
My time is done; I must move on

The life I've lived has really shone
With colour, love, and laughter
Now I've left this worldly throng
For His promised peace hereafter

I know you'll miss my cheery face
My loving words and warm embrace
But I am free from the trouble and strife
To rest in God till my heavenly new life

One day I hope to see you there
With love and peace in light-filled air
Then once again we'll be together
Never to be separated forever

The Promise of Eternal Life

It's usual to mourn for a loved one who has died. However, if you have claimed the promises of Jesus Christ you will live forever upon the return of our King. It's never too late to find Him. He will raise us from the dead just as He rose to show us immortality, and He is coming back for us whether we are dead or still living. The best thing in this life is to prepare for death. This way, we live life to the fullest, never knowing when our time is up but ever ready for His return.

Imagine our dearly loved ones who have already died being alive again and able to live together with us forever. Amazing, exciting, and wonderful! Why be sad about death when there are so many beautiful promises?

> Truly I tell you, all this will come on this generation. 'Jerusalem, Jerusalem, you who kill the prophets and stone those sent to you, how often I have longed to gather your children together, as a hen gathers her chicks under her wings, and you were not willing.' Matthew 23:36–37, NIV

> 'Never again will they hunger; never again will they thirst. The sun will not beat down on them,' nor any scorching heat. For the Lamb at the centre of the throne will be their shepherd; 'he will lead them to springs of living water.' 'And God will wipe away every tear from their eyes.' Revelation 7:16–17, NIV

> And I heard a loud voice from the throne saying, 'Look! God's dwelling place is now among the people, and he will dwell with them. They will be his people, and God himself will be with them and be their God. "He will wipe every tear from their eyes. There will be no more death" or mourning or crying or pain, for the old order of things has passed away.' He who was seated on the throne said, 'I am making everything new!' Then he said, 'Write this down, for these words are trustworthy and true.' He said to me: 'It is done. I am the Alpha and the Omega, the Beginning and the End. To the thirsty I will give water without cost from the spring of the water of life.' Revelation 21:3–6, NIV

The Mind of RAM

Oh, how one thought does prompt and ignite
Urgent desires to creatively write.
The powerful pen begins the fight,
Explaining my world in just the right light

The words flow out from my muse within
Can't stop before they begin again.
In my mind, no rest, just flows along,
Only ceasing when there's a block to the song.

A poem, a verse, a limerick or rhyme,
My mind's so full most of the time.
Let me dip in the treasures, go deep
To release these creations I cannot keep.

To make my thoughts and feelings known,
No longer to claim, now have others own.
I'll take my words out and put them on paper.
Creative writing is quite a caper.

Words loosely stored in books and on papers,
Written down, not lost, much safer.
Most are created in black and white.
I pray you will read the words I write.

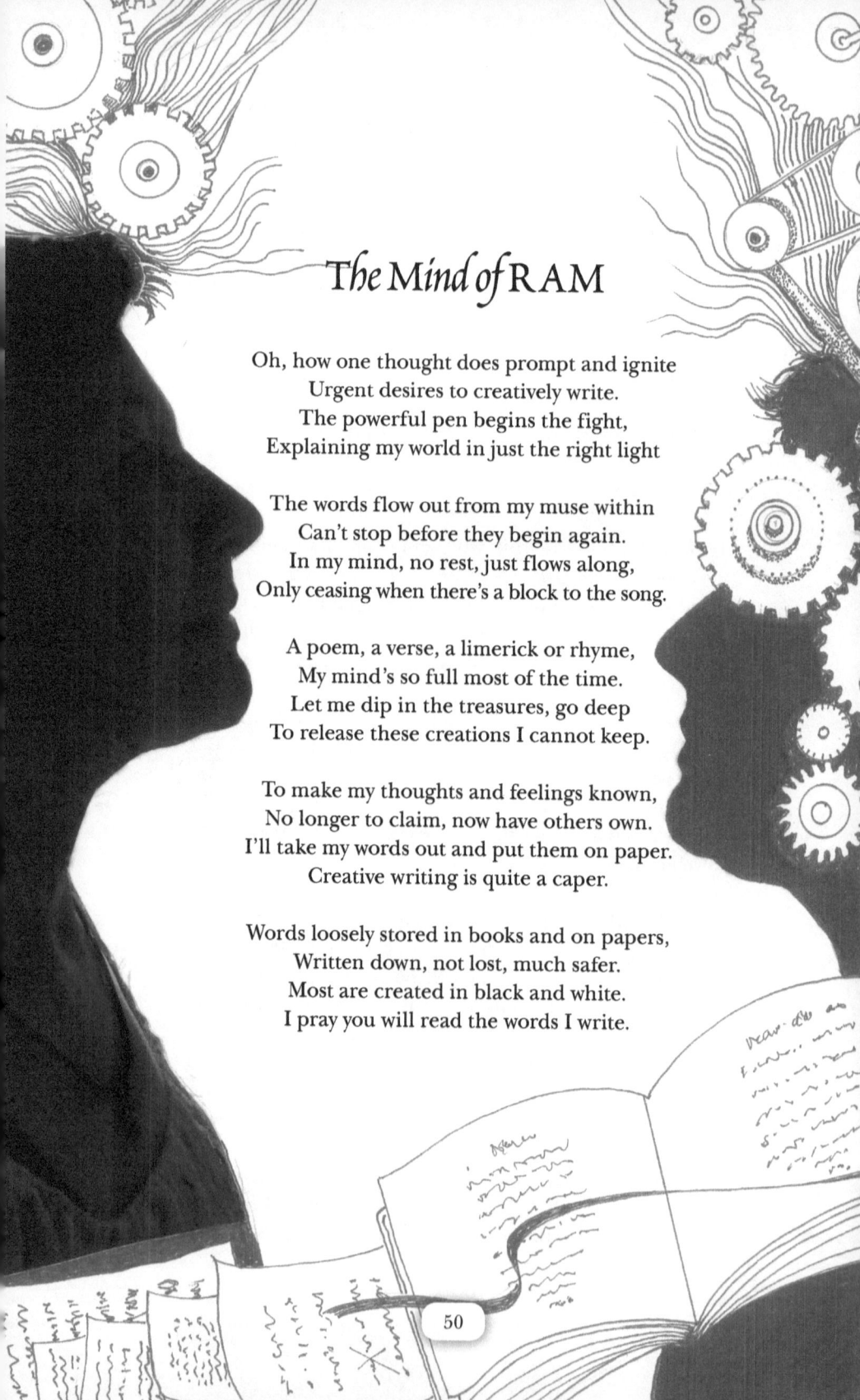

Wonderfully Made

> 'Love the Lord your God with all your heart and with all your soul and with all your mind.' This is the first and greatest commandment. Matthew 22:37–38, NIV

Our minds are quite amazingly made, and if we don't consciously take control of our thoughts, they can lead us astray. What we read, see, study, and experience all influence and direct the way of our thoughts. When we become determined to proceed in a difficult direction, it takes our willpower and mind's strength to keep us on track.

God knows us. He created us. He can lead and guide us in difficult choices when we feel that all our strength is gone, and before we can even think about asking God for help, He already knows. What confidence I have in this thought.

> Before they call I will answer; while they are yet speaking I will hear. Isaiah 65:24, ESV

> Therefore, I urge you, brothers and sisters, in view of God's mercy, to offer your bodies as a living sacrifice, holy and pleasing to God—this is your true and proper worship. Do not conform to the pattern of this world but be transformed by the renewing of your mind. Then you will be able to test and approve what God's will is—his good, pleasing and perfect will. Romans 12:1–2, NIV

If we decide to become followers of Christ, it is our responsibility to fill our minds with wonderful, loving thoughts to become the type of followers Christ wants, and our reward here on this earth is the peace that God imparts to us. This peace is not of the world. There is no understanding it. When everything is literally falling apart, we can say 'God is in control' and know that there's a new start every day. Leave the old cares behind. Consciously give all your worries to Christ, and you must believe He will carry them for you.

About the Author

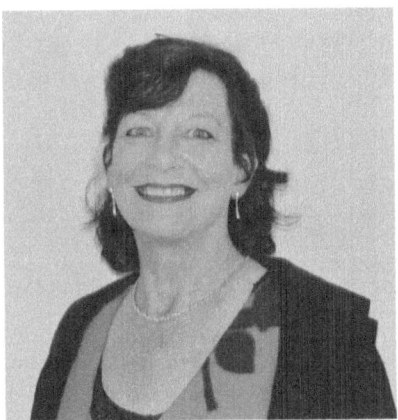

Creativity, deep spirituality, and a real passion for life have been the hallmarks of Robyn's personality throughout her life.

As the second child and first girl in a family of eight children, responsibility and care of others has forged this personality into a force to be reckoned with.

Fun-loving and adventuresome, Robyn is usually first one up on the dance floor, always ready for a good laugh and the retelling of a fabulous tale!

Robyn's journey has not been an easy one. Many of her siblings (including herself) have been involved in separate grievous motor vehicle accidents (never as the driver), resulting in serious trauma, most of which are still causing life-changing disabilities to the present day.

The burden which fell to Robyn to carry during these times and during her own continuing cancer battle have been formative in creating an author with insight, strength, compassion, and deep longing to share her strongly held faith in God.

This book of verse and devotion come straight from the heart of this passionate, devoted, and deeply spiritual person.

I challenge anyone to read through this work without being moved.

Scripture References for the Devotionals

D1. Sing Praise to the King of the Universe: Psalm 47, NIV; Psalm 4:3, NIV; Psalm 66:1–4, NIV; James 5:13, NIV.

D2. Peace at the Centre: John 14:27, NIV, Colossians 3:15, GNT; Philippians 4:6–7, NIV; Proverbs 14:30; Isaiah 26:3, NIV; Psalm 85:10–11, NIV,1 Peter 310-11, NIV

D3. Surrender All: Psalm 31:14–15, NRSV; 2 Chronicles 16:9, NIV; Philippians 4:6–7, NIV; Job 42:1–3, NIV; Galatians 2:20, NIV.

D4. God's Handwriting: Psalm 19:1, CEV; Psalm 8:1–9, NIV; Hebrews 8:10, NIV.

D5. Give God the Glory: Psalm 147:1, The Message; Isaiah 30:21, NIV; Psalm 34:1–4, NIV; 1 Chronicles 29:10–13, NIV; Revelation 4:12, NIV.

D6. God Is Everywhere: Psalm 139:5, The Message; Isaiah 30:21, NIV; Romans 8:38–39, NIV; Proverbs 3:24–26, NIV; Deuteronomy 12:7, NIV.

D7 and D8 are full-page illustrations.

D9. Masks Off: 1 Samuel 16:7, CEV; Psalm 86:11–13; Philippians 4:4–9, NIV; Psalm 46:1–4.

D10. What God's Love Means: Zephaniah 3:17, NIV; 1 John 4:9–11, NIV; Ephesians 2:4–5, NIV; Psalm 86:7, NIV; Romans 8:37–39, NIV;

D11. Everlasting Steams: Isaiah 44:3–5, NIV; Amos 5:24, NIV.

D12. Ascribe Glory to the Lord: Psalm 29:1–4, NIV.

D13. See the Light: John 8:12, The Message; Isaiah 9:2, The Message; Colossians 2:8–9, NIV; Matthew 24:23–24, NIV; Colossians 2:18, NIV; Isaiah 9:2, NIV; 1 John 1:5, NIV; Isaiah 60:19, NIV; 1 John 1:5–9 NIV.

D14. Taming the Tongue: Proverbs 15:4, Let God Be True; James 3:3–12, NIV; Proverbs 18:21, NSV; Psalm 34:13, NSV; Psalm 141:13, NIV; Proverbs 18:7–10, NIV; Matthew 12:33–36, NIV; 1 Peter 3:10–11.

D15. From the Lord Comes Deliverance: 1 Peter 5:8, NIV; Psalm 143:9–10, NIV; Daniel 6:27, NIV; Psalm 3:8, NIV; Psalm 18:2, NIV; Psalm 72:12–14, NIV; Proverbs 3:5–6, NIV; Hebrews 2:13, NIV.

D16. The Want of Money: Ecclesiastes 5:10–11, NIV; Ezekiel 7:19, NIV; Deuteronomy 15:10, NIV; Hebrews 13:5, NIV; 1 Timothy 6:10, NIV; 1 Timothy 3:2–3, NIV; 1 Peter 5:2, NIV; Matthew 6:31–33, NIV; Philippians 4:11–13, NIV.

D17. Hold On to God: Psalm 34:17–18, NKJV; 2 Corinthians 4:8–9, NIV; Hebrews 13:6, NIV; Psalm 61:1–2, NIV; Psalm 63:1–7, NIV; 2 Samuel 22:1–4, NIV; Psalm 17:7–8, NKJV; reference to Psalm 17:6–9.

D18. God Will Rescue Us: reference to Daniel 6:20, Daniel 3:16–18, NIV; Psalm 143:9, NIV; Colossians 1:13, NIV; Joshua 1:5, NIV; Psalm 31:2, NIV; Psalm 10:17–18, NIV; Psalm 69:14–15, NIV; Galatians 1:3–5, NIV.

D19. Spiritually Strong: Galatians 6:7–8, NIV; Isaiah 30:21, NIV; Romans 12:2, GNT; Galatians 5:22–23, NIV; Joshua 1:9, NIV; Philippians 4:13, NIV; Isaiah 40:29–31, NIV; Psalm 138:1–3, ESV.

D20. Stand Tall with Faith in Your Heart: Hebrews 11:1–2, NLT; Isaiah 11:6–9, NIV; Romans 8:6, NIV; Psalm 145:14–19, KJ 2000; Isaiah 41:10, NIV.

D21. I Am the Door: Revelation 3:20, NIV; Luke 11:9–10, NIV; John 10:7, NIV; Colossians 4:3, NIV; Revelation 3:7–8, NIV.

D22. Spiritual Armour: Ephesians 6:10–18, NIV; Luke 4:18–19, NIV; Isaiah 40:29, NIV;

D23. Remember Others: Luke 6:30–38, NIV; Luke 6:35–36, NIV; Proverbs 25:21–22, NIV; Colossians 3:12–14, NIV.

D24. The Promise of Eternal Life, Matthew 23:36–37, NIV; Revelation 7:16–17, NIV; Revelation 21:3–6, NIV; 1 John 4:7–12; Isaiah 26:19, NIV.

D25. Wonderfully Made: Matthew 22:37–38, NIV; Isaiah 65:24, ESV; Romans 12:1–2, NIV; Philippians 4:4–9, NIV; Psalm 119:27, NIV; Psalm 145:5, NIV; Isaiah 52:7, NIV.

NIV: New International Version
NKJV: New King James Version
GNT: Good News Translation
ESV: English Standard Version
NLT: New Living translation
KJ 2000: King James 2000

General Index

A

Abednego (Hebrew man) 37
Aldrin, Buzz 9
angels 13, 21, 27
armour, spiritual 45, 55
Armstrong, Neil 9

B

blessings 5, 13, 23, 31, 38

C

cancer vii, ix, 1, 11, 53
compassion 1, 6, 38, 47, 53
cross 2, 20, 43

D

Daniel (Hebrew prophet) 31
David (king of Judah and Israel) 35
death 13, 21, 29, 31, 37, 41, 49
deception 26, 28, 38
deliverance 31, 55
demons 13, 21
devil 8, 31

E

enemies 31, 47

F

faith vii, 1, 7-8, 12, 18, 20-1, 33, 35, 37, 41
  foundation of 21
friendship 46

G

God 1-3, 5, 7-9, 11-13, 19-23, 25-7, 29-40, 43-5, 47-9, 51
  armour of 30, 44
  grace of 26, 44
  grand design of 8
  handwriting of 8-9, 54
  light of 27
  love of vii, 5, 13, 21, 32, 34, 40, 54
  presence of 5, 13, 19
  wonders of 9
God, Word of 34, 36
grace 8, 11, 18, 26, 36, 42-4
grief vii, 32-3, 36, 47

H

heaven vii, 9, 21, 31, 38
hell 29
Holy Spirit 1, 7, 12, 22-3, 25-6, 30-1, 37, 39, 41, 44-5
  sword of 44-5

I

illness 7, 12, 18, 20

J

Jerusalem 43, 49
Jesus Christ 5, 7, 13, 19, 21, 31, 49
  death of 35
  return of 41, 49
  sacrifice of 2

L

lion of judah 44

M

Mardi Gras Museum 19
masks 18-19, 54
Meshach (Hebrew man) 37
money 16, 32-4, 55
moon landing 9
mourning 48-9

N

Nebuchadnezzar (king of Babylon) 37
New Orleans 19

P

peace 1-3, 5, 18-19, 23-4, 29, 32, 34, 39, 44-5, 51
Power of the Mask 19
praises 2-3, 11, 29, 34, 54

prayers vii, 5, 7, 10, 13, 19, 34-5, 45, 47

S

salvation 31, 44-5
Satan 31, 40, 44-5
Shadrach (Hebrew man) 37
sins 21, 26, 30, 38, 40
soul 2-4, 6, 12-13, 22, 24, 26, 30, 32, 40, 46

T

temptation 12, 30
tongue 5, 28-9, 36, 54
   wholesome 29

W

wisdom 8, 26, 33

Scriptural Index

Deuteronomy:
 12:7 *54*
 15:10 *55*
Joshua:
 1:5 *55*
 1:9 *55*
1 Samuel:
 16:7 *19*, 54
2 Samuel:
 22:1–4 *55*
2 Chronicles 16:9 *7, 54*
John:
 8:12 *27, 54*
 10:7 *43, 55*
Job 42:1–3 *54*
Psalm:
 3:8 *31, 55*
 4:3 *54*
 8:1–9 *54*
 10:17–18 *55*
 17:6–9 *55*
 17:7–8 *55*
 18:2 *31, 55*
 19:1 *9, 54*
 29:1–4 *25, 54*
 31:14–15 *7, 54*
 31:2 *55*
 34:1–4 *54*
 34:13 *29, 54*
 34:17–18 *35, 55*
 46:1–4 *54*
 47 *3, 54*
 61:1–2 *35, 55*
 63:1–7 *55*
 66:1–4 *54*
 69:14–15 *55*
 72:12–14 *31, 55*
 85:10–11 *54*
 86:11–13 *54*
 86:7 *54*
 119:27 *55*
 138:1–3 *55*
 139:5 *13, 54*
 141:13 *54*
 143:9 *31, 55*
 143:9–10 *31, 55*
 145:14–19 *55*
 145:5 *55*
 147:1 *11, 54*
Proverbs:
 3:24–26 *13, 54*
 3:5–6 *31, 55*
 14:30 *54*
 15:4 *29, 54*
 18:7–10 *54*
 18:21 *29, 54*
 25:21–22 *47, 55*
Ecclesiastes 5:10–11 *55*
Isaiah:
 9:2 *27, 54*
 11:6–9 *41, 55*
 26:3 *54*
 26:19 *55*
 30:21 *39, 54, 55*
 40:29 *55*
 40:29–31 *55*
 41:10 *55*
 44:3–5 *23, 54*
 52:7 *55*
 60:19 *27, 54*
 65:24 *51, 55*
Ezekiel 7:19 *33, 55*
Daniel:
 3:16–18 *37, 55*
 6:20 *37, 55*
 6:27 *31, 55*
Amos 5:24 *54*
Zephaniah 3:17 *54*

Matthew:
  6:31–33 *55*
  12:33–36 *54*
  22:37–38 *51, 55*
  23:36–37 *49, 55*
  24:23–24 *27, 54*
Luke:
  4:18–19 *55*
  6:30–38 *55*
  6:35–36 *47, 55*
  11:9–10 *43, 55*
Romans:
  8:6 *41, 55*
  8:37–39 *54*
  8:38–39 *13, 54*
  12:1–2 *51, 55*
  12:2 *39, 55*
2 Corinthians 4:8–9 *55*
Galatians:
  1:3–5 *55*
  2:20 *54*
  5:22–23 *39, 55*
Ephesians:
  2:4–5 *21, 54*
  6:10–18 *45, 55*
Philippians:
  4:4–9 *54, 55*
  4:6–7 *54*
  4:11–13 *55*
  4:13 *55*
Colossians:
  1:13 *55*
  2:8–9 *27, 54*
  2:18 *27, 54*
  3:12–14 *55*
  3:15 *5*
  4:3 *43, 55*
1 Timothy:
  3:2–3 *33, 55*
  6:10 *33, 55*
Hebrews:
  2:13 *31, 55*

  8:10 *54*
  11:1–2 *41, 55*
  13:5 *33, 55*
  13:6 *35, 55*
James:
  3:3–12 *29, 54*
  5:13 *54*
1 Peter:
  3:10–11 *29, 54*
  5:2 *55*
  5:8 *55*
1 John:
  1:5 *27, 54*
  1:5–9 *54*
  4:7–12 *55*
  4:9–11 *54*
Revelation:
  3:7–8 *55*
  3:20 *55*
  4:12 *54*
  7:16–17 *49, 55*
  21:3–6 *49, 55*

www.ingramcontent.com/pod-product-compliance
Lightning Source LLC
Chambersburg PA
CBHW031543210526
45464CB00003B/1123